RESCUED
From Drugs to Jesus

Courtney Kacer

RESCUED
From Drugs to Jesus
Copyright © 2024 by Courtney Kacer

Library of Congress Control Number: 2024910885
ISBN-13: Paperback: 978-1-64749-977-8
          Epub: 978-1-64749-978-5

Printed in the United States of America

GoToPublish LLC
1-888-337-1724
www.gotopublish.com
info@gotopublish.com

Contents

Prologue
PURE DARKNESS

Turn away from me so I can have a moment's joy before I go to the place of no return, to the land of gloom and utter darkness, to the land of deepest night, of utter darkness and disorder, where even the light is like darkness.

—Job 10:20–22

I never thought in a million years that I would be here in this place—a place so dark and cold. As I slowly walked through this house, it was like watching a scene from a movie. There were half-burned candles flickering to light the way, their wax dripping down the side onto the worn furniture. There didn't appear to be any electricity. The house was full of people sprawled out over the couches and floors, some seemingly lost in their own thoughtful bliss, while others fidgeted and seemed preoccupied with who knew what. Many just appeared to be wasting away, with a dull, dead look in their eyes. It was dirty and unkempt. I was standing in the middle of a crack house, taking in the surroundings and knowing deep down I was not supposed to be there.

I was so scared; I was trembling inside, but I couldn't show the sheer panic I was feeling, or I might put myself in danger. There were about twenty people around me, and straight in front of me stood my friend, smoking crack with a random drug dealer.

RESCUED

I had been around drugs before and had even used them, but never had I been around crack, let alone in a real crack house. My reality did not fully comprehend that there could even be places like this. Why would anyone want to live this way? This was something only on TV or in the movies, right?

All I wanted to do was run, run as fast as I could away from here, but I stood frozen, paralyzed. Time just stood still in that moment. Why couldn't I take control of my body and just move? I had no idea who these people were, nor did I know how they were going to react if I did decide to leave, and even then, did I want to leave my friends and walk away by myself in the middle of the night? Not only did I not know where we were, but I also knew we were not in a safe neighborhood. A thousand questions, a thousand thoughts running through my mind.

I decided to stay because I was with two of my guy friends, my very big guy friends. They would protect me if anything went wrong. The guy I was dating, and I were not even supposed to go into the house. We were to wait for our friend out in the car, who was going to be only five minutes. After forty-five minutes of waiting, we decided to go in and make sure everything was okay. I did not want to go in, but I did not want to stay in the car by myself either.

As it turned out, our friend was okay, but the drug dealer, to my dismay, decided to invite us to have a seat and join him. I reluctantly sat on the dirt-stained couch, in hopes that we would leave before anything happened, you know, that I could not take back. The dealer turned his attention to me, a pretty nineteen-year-old girl who was not like any of the other women who normally hung out at a place like this. My heart began to pound out of my chest, and I grabbed my boyfriend's hand and squeezed it.

He seemed to be very nice, and he asked me if I would like a hit. I told him, "No, thank you." I wanted to tell him that I did drugs but not crack. Never crack. Instead, I just sat there. He must have sensed that I had never tried it and asked me, more as a statement than a question, "You have never smoked crack before, have you?"

"No. I have not," I said, all while trying to sound like it was no big deal. Without missing a beat, he explained that it was the best feeling in the world and insisted that I try it. "You should try it. Here, I'll show you."

My mind was racing. What was I to do? He was quite scary to me, and crack was not something that I really wanted to get into. But even though I was scared, even with the nagging feeling that I should not, I tried crack for the first time. Not only did I try it, but I did it all night long until there was no more left to smoke and no more money to spend for the night.

Chapter 1
MY CHILDHOOD

For in every adult there dwells the child that was, and in
every child there lies the adult that will be.
—John Connelly, *The Book of Lost Things*

G rowing up in my home was like going on several different
roller coasters. Some of our adventures were very
exciting—full of speed, loops, screams, and laughter. Other
times, it was like that old wooden roller coaster that was bumpy
the whole way through. But no matter what the situation with
my family, we got through it together. When I was about
twelve, we went on a cross-country road trip from California
to Ohio. My father, in response to anything that would happen,
especially negative stuff, would always say, "Remember, kids, it
is all part of the adventure." It was his way of helping us to stay
positive no matter what happened. To this day, we still quote
him through the good times and the bad.

I grew up in a Christian home and am the oldest of four
children, two boys and two girls. Let's just say our house was
rarely quiet. We lived on the end of a cul-de-sac with lots
of kids our age. There were always kids coming in and out
of our house. We spent many nights with the neighborhood
kids playing games outside, with not a care in the world until
Mom would yell out the front door, "Dinnertime!" Honestly,

there couldn't have been a better neighborhood in which to grow up. I will forever remember the two-story house in Tracy during my adolescent years. We would try to get in as much trouble as we could, whether it be water fights in the house with my dad—yes, my dad—or jumping off our roof onto our big trampoline and then into our pool (we only did that one when the parents weren't home). We would even play hide-and-seek in the house with my dad, where his favorite place to hide was the laundry chute that went between the second and first floors. It amazed me there were not more trips to the emergency room than there were.

My parents loved to have family time. It was much easier to get us all together when we were younger, but I remember TGIF, where we would make pizza, popcorn, and soda and watch all the family shows that were on every Friday night. Those were the days when *Full House*, *Family Matters*, and other family-oriented shows were on. It was the only night we were allowed to stay up until 10:00 p.m. each week. We would have game and movie nights, and for the most part, we would watch football together on Sundays. Go, 49ers! One of my fondest memories is when my dad spent several nights reading *Narnia* to all of us kids. We would race upstairs and jump on his bed, and he would read a chapter to us every night. I didn't think much of it then, but looking back on it now, my parents made sure we had special unique moments to remember. Not only did we have family time, but my parents would spend individual time with each of us separately, as well, making sure each of us kids knew that our parents loved us. My dad would spend time with me practicing basketball, and my mom and I would spend special days shopping and sharing our love for shoes. My parents weren't perfect, but they came close, always making sure that we knew we were loved.

> Follow God's example, therefore, as dearly loved
> children and walk in the way of love, just as Christ
> loved us and gave himself up for us as a fragrant
> offering and sacrifice to God. (Ephesians 5:1–2)

It was important to my parents to teach us the morals and values of their Christian faith. We went to church every Sunday, and as a family, we were heavily involved. I remember my dad would usher, and my mom would play piano. All of us kids would be in the children's plays during the holidays and were involved in all the youth groups. Church was a fun place to go. All our friends were there, and it was a constructive place for us to be.

When you grow up in the church your whole life, your spiritual beliefs tend to be your parents' beliefs until you accept them as your own. I believe there is a moment in your life where an individual makes the choice to have a personal relationship with Christ. Some people make that choice from very early on and live their faith throughout the full cycle of their life, maturing spiritually as they get older. Some people may push away from the faith and church altogether, never adopting it. Or you can be like me, wavering back and forth in uncertainty until adulthood.

I loved going to church, but it was primarily because of the people who were there and the relationships I had with my friends. I went to church because we went as a family and it was fun, but not because I wanted to learn more about God. There were times when I was more apt to study God's Word, and that was when I was interested in or dating someone. But as I was getting into my senior year in high school, I started to push away from the church and my faith. The pleasures of this world seemed to be a lot more enticing, and I wanted to explore beyond the realms of the boundaries within which I was raised.

But what was it in my personality that caused me to drift? I knew there was a God, and I knew all the different stories of the Bible, but for some reason, my heart was not connecting to the knowledge I had obtained throughout the years.

My mom once told me that I loved attention growing up. I would intentionally seek it out anywhere I went. Here is what my mom said, in her own words: "When Courtney was about three years old, we were walking in the mall. We began to pass an electronics store that was advertising televisions in the window, and there was an aerobics or dance program being played. This caught Courtney's attention, and she stopped and started mimicking what was on the television. I have to admit it was the cutest thing. People stopped and made comments on how cute she was, and it was clear that, even at that tender age, she recognized the attention and doubled her efforts, all the while grinning from ear to ear."

Sadly, in the long run, that type of attention, for my personality, just turned into a stronger desire for me to be selfish. It was all about me—what I wanted to do, my looks, my clothes. I was definitely into myself when I was growing up. Honestly, I really don't know how much of that is normal for a teenage girl and how much is not. But I do remember my family—mainly my brothers and my sister—would make fun of me because every time I walked by a mirror, any mirror, I would look at myself to make sure that my hair was in place and that I looked up to the standards I had made for myself. On a side note, if only I knew all the style tricks I know now. I look back at some of my style choices back then, and I ask myself, *What was I thinking?* But I digress.

Because of my selfish nature, I was very manipulative, especially in my teen years. I would actually weigh my possible punishments against the things I wanted to do that my parents had prohibited. Was sneaking out of the house to go to a party worth two weeks of grounding? If the punishment was worth it, I would do it; if it wasn't, I wouldn't do it. In my dad's own words, "Courtney was quite the master when it came to defying the rules. It wasn't that she was trying to be clever and hide what she was doing or even come up with some conceived 'misunderstanding' of what the rules were. No, for her, it was quite simple. If she wanted to do the forbidden acts badly enough, she would suck it up and just take the punishment. I remember one time telling her that she could not ride her bike past a certain point in the neighborhood. The punishment was a spanking with the famous 'board of education' that I had made. She carefully considered the consequences and decided that the pleasure and freedom of going beyond the boundary was worth the pain of the spanking. Needless to say, it required some creative parenting on our part to find consequences that were effective for her."

As he said, it forced them to get creative with some of my punishments. Let's just say I spent a lot of time in my room without any television, and boy, did I love my shows.

On the outside, I projected strong confidence, but on the inside, I was very insecure. Where did that insecurity come from? Honestly, I really don't know. It was probably a combination of things, but the only thing I could think of was kids bullying me when I was little. I know that I am not the only one who suffered in this way, but when it is happening, it feels that way. It amazes me how cruel kids can be and how it was torture going through the cruelty of the verbal attacks. But somehow, I still wanted to be part of that very same group. Everyone wants to belong to something, to feel accepted. The kids would chase me, making pig noises and grunting, calling me a pig because my nose is a little turned up. Or in junior high, when I had bad acne, they would ask me how I could have chicken pox again when I just had them last week.

It seems in today's culture that bullying is even worse to the point that kids are committing suicide or having suicidal thoughts so early in their lives, before they have the maturity to know who they are and that they are worth so much more. Any bullying that is done shows the other person's insecurity and normally has nothing to do with the value of any individual. There has to be something more we can do in our schools and at home to help combat bullying, but that is for another time.

Whatever confidence I had as a little girl dancing in the malls was washed away every time I went to school. Each time I did anything, going forward, I would analyze the situation over and over, worried that my actions would look stupid. I had this constant fear of how people would think of me, and having that lifelong need for attention and acceptance, I tried to please everyone around me. With this thought process, I was turning into what people wanted me to be instead of becoming my own person. Whatever group I was with would dictate how I changed my personality. I could never seem to get a handle on it, so personality fluctuations and attention-seeking behavior followed me into my early adulthood.

In junior high and high school, I found a constructive outlet for this attention-seeking behavior through sports. I played basketball in junior high and high school, along with volleyball. Playing in games where I could highlight myself alongside a team atmosphere was the perfect setting to complement my desires to be in the limelight. In my senior year in high school, I had the nickname Courtney "From Downtown" Smith. Three-pointers were my specialty. There was one game where I hit five three-pointers in the first half of the basketball game. I was on fire. I had no idea how I made so many, but they just kept going *swish, swish, swish*. The crowd was standing and screaming every time I made a basket. If there is one moment in my life that I would like to do over and over, it would be this moment. All eyes were on what I would do next, and I absolutely loved it. The team walked into the locker room during halftime, and my coach said not to sit down because I would cool off. I was flaming hot. That game, I scored eighteen points, the best game of my life. Every newspaper interviewed me after the game. My parents couldn't stop talking about it. I ended up getting the Athlete of the Week for the county newspaper, Athlete of the Month from the city, and a few other awards that year.

I write this event in detail because it is important to know the feelings that I lived for, the emotion that I constantly longed for, the trigger that would put me over the top. I thrived that night especially, feeling like I was accepted and loved by my peers. That is what I had always wanted from the time I was dancing in the malls, through my teenage years: love and acceptance. I felt I had finally achieved it from my peers. The adrenaline that was running through my veins was an unbelievable feeling. A feeling that would become an addiction, an unhealthy addiction. I was becoming addicted to acceptance and stature.

I read a psychology article that stated this:

> Peer acceptance is measured by the quality rather than the quantity of a child or adolescent's relationships. While the number of friends varies among children and over time as a child develops, peer acceptance is often established as early as preschool. Factors such as physical attractiveness, cultural traits, and disabilities affect the level of peer acceptance, with a child's degree of social competence being the best predictor of peer

acceptance. Children who are peer-accepted or popular have fewer problems in middle and high school, and teens who are peer-accepted have fewer emotional and social adjustment problems as adults." The choices I made were my choices, and I take full responsibility for them, but knowing that the lack of peer acceptance could be a small contributing factor to why my thought process was the way it was is somehow comforting. The biggest struggle we all have is feeling like there is something inherently wrong with us. That we are somehow defective, more so than others. There was some modicum of comfort in feeling like maybe it was not all my fault.[1]

Why I was not accepted in my early childhood is still a mystery to me, but I know that I struggled every day of my life toward acceptance and not rejection. Even though I believe peer acceptance was a factor, I have these nagging thoughts to explain why I felt the need to chase after these feelings when I had such a stable home and a family who loved me and who would do anything for me.

I did not come from a broken home. My parents are still married today, going on forty-three years. They supported me through all my ideas and desires while I was growing up. They went to a lot of my games and cheered for me in the stands. They supported me through the Miss Teen California pageant during my freshman year in high school by taking me to all the interviews and flying me to Southern California for the weekend. They did everything they thought would help me grow and find my identity.

---

1   Psychology Encyclopedia, "Peer Acceptance," accessed January 29, 2024, http://psychology.jrank.org/pages/477/Peer-Acceptance.html#ixzz3OT8zsg3C.

They would not allow me to do things they knew would stunt that growth. They were my parents. My siblings and I fought a lot when we were growing up, but we also had a lot of good times. Looking in from the outside, I imagine we would be the stable family that people would want to join. But I started to brush my family aside in my teen years to go off on a path that would forever change my life.

During my senior year in high school, I started to rebel against my parents. I would make up any excuse not to go to church. The need to be part of the popular crowd was starting to take over. While I played sports, I did everything I needed to do to make sure I could play in the games. But once I played my last game, I felt an even bigger void that I tried to fill. By the time basketball was over, I only had a few more months until I graduated.

I started to hang out with my friends more and to go to parties. These friends liked to drink and smoke. They had the freedom that I never had. I would lie to my parents to go out to these parties, and I started to drink more and more. I was part of the cool crowd, and that was what was filling my sense of loss.

Knowing that you will never play the one thing that you love the most brings this depression and sense of loss that can overtake you. I felt like I had no idea who I was or what I was going to do. I was seventeen and completely lost. Sports had become my identity, and when that was over, I needed a new identity. I had no idea who I was or what I really wanted. More importantly, I had lost the vehicle of popularity that signaled acceptance from my peers.

When it comes to different personalities, I am definitely my father's daughter, which is why I believe my relationship with my dad suffered the most at that time. We argued constantly.

I wanted to go to cosmetology school instead of four years of college, and we fought about that. I wanted to do things that went against the plans my parents had for me, and we fought about that. I was tired of all the rules and boundaries my parents had set for me. I was feeling completely claustrophobic.

I wanted to be free and follow the beat to my own drum and not anyone else's. My parents would give me ultimatums, and I rebelled against those. I was rude to my siblings and treated them with rejection. Nothing was going to stand in the way of me finding myself my own way, with the exception of going to the four-year college. That was the one thing I agreed to do. I could at least move out. As long as I went and finished school, my parents were going to pay for it, which, I realize, now was such an amazing opportunity for me as I know many people do not get that same privilege.

I was accepted to two state colleges, Chico and San Diego State, both on the top-ten list of party schools. I chose to go to San Diego State and promptly moved to the opposite end of the state from my family. Here I was thinking I would go to school, hurry up and get my degree, and start my career. Little did I know that it would be the start of a very dark path over the next few years.

Chapter 2
THE DARK PATH BEGINS

The decision to go to San Diego State was probably not the best one, considering it was labeled as one of the top-ten party schools in the nation. But it was in sunny Southern California and only six hours away from home. I met my roommate on the first day. She was definitely going to be a sorority girl, as she had "partier" written all over her. She was a gorgeous blonde, and I knew that if I hung out with her, I would experience the wild freedom that I so craved. The first night after I said goodbye to my parents, she and I hit the party scene. Everyone was back at school, and parties were everywhere. We went to a few different fraternity houses, and I had a few drinks, but I was so out of my element I didn't really know what to do. I remember going back to my dorm room early and going to bed. I wanted my freedom, but I was definitely outside the bubble I had been living in for so many years—that bubble that my parents and I had created growing up. It was a whole different world full of kids my age, most of whom were on their own for the first time. It was about to get crazy.

The next day, my roommate told me she met a bunch of guys at the fraternity house right across our dorms, and we were all going to the beach. It was a great day full of friendly interactions, and for the first time in a very long time, I felt like I was part of the "cool" group. It was also the start of a downward spiral that would take me years to overcome. I would go to all their parties and hang out with them on different nights. We were their "girls." I would get drunk every night and miss class about 50 percent of the time, which put me right onto academic probation after the first semester of school.

With the desire for love and acceptance that I so craved, I began to look for that special relationship. And the one thing that I thought I would preserve until marriage; I ended up giving up one night while completely intoxicated—my virginity. Over the next week, I realized that the man I gave my body to had no interest in me or a relationship. He was just having fun. The sad part? I was more disappointed that he didn't like me enough to be in a relationship rather than the loss of my virginity. Even sadder? I got over it quickly and turned to the next person who started to show interest in me, and then on to the next person, and on to the next person. Everyone I met was connected to this fraternity house. I soon was beginning to get a reputation as the girl who was easy. Growing up, I never wanted to be "that girl," but that is what I became.

I wanted love so ferociously that I was willing to give up the things that would give me a great man and a lasting love. I gave up my integrity, my respect, and my dignity. The love that I was searching for was a forever type of love. I wanted to settle down, have kids, and live the normal life with a family of my own, but I was never going to get there by disrespecting myself and disrespecting God.

I was reading a book called *Lady in Waiting* a couple of years ago, and it stated, "Too many women grow up believing that the inconsolable ache in her heart is for 'a man.' To love a man, get married, and then have children is thought to be the only script that will satisfy her heart's deepest longing. But no man, woman, or child can appease this longing; it can only be satisfied by the ultimate Bridegroom, Christ Jesus. *Lady in Waiting* is not about finding the right man but being the right woman." I will be talking more about this later in the book, but the point is that at this time in my life, I was far from the mark of what God wanted me to be. Looking back, I could see how God was weeping for me, knowing that my decisions were putting me farther and farther from Him.

This season brought on a deep depression in which my heart was breaking over and over, and my self-worth was dwindling with each passing day. My heart had a huge void that I was continuing to fill with everything it didn't need, with a continual feed of darkness that kept feeding the beast of depression.

I didn't want to go to class; I didn't know what I wanted to do with my life. I would sleep all day and then get up and go to parties, drinking until I stumbled home or throwing up in toilets and passing out on bathroom floors. Hangovers were an almost everyday thing. Part of me wanted to just curl up and not wake up again.

Academic probation was a bit of a wake-up call. My second semester, my roommate moved into her sorority. I had the dorm room all to myself, and I quickly became friends with a different group of people. I was going to class a little bit more, but more out of fear of what my parents would do if I was kicked out of school. I wanted to get a job so that I had my own money to go out and do different things. My parents told me no. They did not want me to work so I could focus on school. What did my parents know?

I went out and got a job anyway. I have always been very independent, and if I earned my own money, my parents couldn't control the decisions of what I used it on. The money at my new job was good, at least for an eighteen-year-old. I started working a little bit more than part-time. I was good at my job, and it started to take some of the depressive thoughts away, but I was still going out and drinking like it was my oxygen and I needed it to breathe.

My new group of friends was my navy friends whom I met in Tijuana, Mexico, in a club one night. My focus switched, and I stopped going to all the fraternity parties, but I didn't learn anything. This group also loved to drink, and I took the bad habits and decisions I was making and just redirected these to them. On the weekends, we would get together and play drinking games.

Although I went to more classes, I hardly studied, and I did not do well on tests. By the time my first year was over, I had failed some of my classes, and my academic probation became a reality. I was no longer accepted at San Diego State. I was kicked out of college. Who would have thought that I would have drifted so far off the path that my parents wanted for me or, better yet, the path God wanted for me? Normal kids who had the opportunity to go to college would have at least had the responsibility and discipline to get through four years of school, even if they did go out and have a little fun.

There I was, kicked out of school and still not really caring about what I was going to do in my future. I was just living in the moment without a care in the world. My best friend and I wanted to move into an apartment off-campus. Living in the dorms was an experience but not something you necessarily wanted to do for more than a year, and I really did not have a choice.

It was time for us to spread our wings a little more. I was able to talk my parents into helping with the rent as long as I enrolled in a junior college to continue taking classes and to get back on track. I wish I could remember the name of that college so that I could tell you how much I was really focused on improving my life and getting it back on track. Clearly, that was not the case. But I did have an apartment of my own, a job in which I was making my own money, and a little more freedom.

My time with my navy friends seemed to drift as I broke up with the guy I was briefly seeing, and a new group of friends came into play. They were a group of people that I looked up to: cool and awesome. They liked me, and I felt part of something, just like with every other group of friends I had previously. But with every new setting, a whole new pool of possibilities presented itself, refreshing my sense of self-worth and wholeness.

We had house parties in which only the group of close friends would be able to climb the roof and look down at about two hundred people in the backyard, all having a blast. I really did enjoy that time. I felt genuinely befriended more with this group of friends than I did with all my friends during my first year of college. However, it was this group of friends that eventually got me into using Ecstasy. I was okay with drinking heavily, but I never really thought that I would do what I considered "hard-core" drugs. I smoked marijuana a few times a week, but I thought that was okay and that was the limit. But that strong relationship I had with this group of friends made me want to do the same thing that all of them were doing, to experience the euphoria that they were in.

I wish I could say that I hated the feelings that came along with the use of Ecstasy, but I didn't. I loved it. For someone who constantly sought love and attention, this was the perfect drug. It is what we used to call the love drug. Everything you touched made you feel wanted and welcomed. It brought our friendships closer, and it was a feeling out of this world. In fact, I used Ecstasy so much that I found I had to take double the dose just to get that same high. I wanted that feeling over and over. We would go to raves and have rave parties at home, where we would have about twenty to thirty people over. I felt on top of the world.

The problem, though, was that when I came down off the drug, reality would set in. I would have to go to school and work, and I still didn't have a steady boyfriend. I was not close to my family, as I had pushed them as far away from me as I could. I felt alone. I started to feel more and more depressed when I was sober, so I would continue to drink, smoke marijuana, and take Ecstasy pills, trying to drown out all the ugliness. The more I didn't have to deal with reality, the better. I was so far from God and so lost, yet I continued to go deeper down into a muddy pit and slowly sinking into quicksand.

I was still looking for love in all the wrong places, and there wasn't a prospect in sight. My life consisted of absolutely nothing of value. I couldn't even tell you who I was or what I wanted at that point. I was still trying to find my way. My parents could do no right. My moods were all over the place and starting to be a bit of Jekyll and Hyde. I think if I had seen a psychiatrist, they could have diagnosed me with being bipolar, but looking back, it was the drugs. I would be happy one moment, depressed the next, and then angry that something wasn't going right. No wonder no one wanted to date me long-term. I thought I was cool by doing drugs and drinking. I was proud that I was able to hold my alcohol better than most people could. But the reality was that I was not the person that I wanted to be or the person a man deserved to have as a girlfriend. During all this, I was constantly thinking about change. What could I do to change my circumstances but still have control over the direction of my life? I didn't want to go home. That would admit that I failed. And there was no way that that was going to happen. Failure was not an option.

As I am writing this and going through the timeline of my life, I can't help but relate to Alice in Wonderland. As she was going through the different challenges that she faced in chasing the White Rabbit, she chose to take pills, drink liquids, and eat different cakes to change her size to fit through different doors and to get to where she was trying to go. That applied to my life. I would meet different groups of people, and I would conform myself and my personality to fit that setting so that I would be accepted.

Just like Alice had no idea where she was going, neither did I. We were both blindly following the curiosity of the circumstances in front of us just to find that we were in a world that we did not know. I was creating my own Alice in Wonderland full of Mad Hatters, potions, mushrooms, and all the other wonderland items just so I could find love and feel complete. At that time of my life, I had no idea where to go. I wasn't thinking long-term, only about what was going to give me that temporary satisfaction.

> "Would you tell me, please, which way I ought to go from here?"
> "That depends a good deal on where you want to get to."
> "I don't much care where—"
> "Then it doesn't matter which way you go."
> (Lewis Carroll, *Alice's Adventures in Wonderland*)

The problem is it should always matter which way we go, as the decisions we make have either blessings or consequences that, more often than not, impact other people.

Those who live according to the flesh have their minds set on what the flesh desires; but those who live in accordance with the Spirit have their minds set on what the Spirit desires. The mind governed by the flesh is death, but the mind governed by the Spirit is life and peace. The mind governed by the flesh is hostile to God; it does not submit to God's law, nor can it do so. Those who are in the realm of the flesh cannot please God. (Romans 8:5–8)

My heart was hardening to the point where it was going to be very hard for me to find my way back to the light. I was living for the flesh of this world and not by the spirit. Instead of stopping to reflect on where I wanted to go, I relied on my spontaneous reflexes and only saw what I wanted at that moment. And that was a whole new setting. San Diego was just not where I wanted to be anymore. This season of my life had run its course. I craved something new and exciting that would pull me out of this fog.

My cousin was getting married in Florida at this time, and she asked me to be her maid of honor. I was so excited to see her and meet all her friends and to be a part of her special day. I took a week's vacation in Florida. I had a lot of fun getting to reconnect with my cousin and enjoying the life that she had built in Florida and the different culture. I met a bunch of people, and of course, I met a guy whom I connected with the first day there. I didn't think it was going to go anywhere since I lived in California, but I had so much fun that I quickly decided to move there.

I remember writing my parents a letter to tell them that I was dropping out of school and moving to Florida to be on my own. I knew they wouldn't approve, and I wanted to make sure I got everything I had to say out in the open without them trying to talk me out of it. I read the letter, and I think they were speechless for a few minutes.

> Courtney told her mother and I about her desire to drop out of school and move to Florida. We were frustrated with her. She wanted to quit just six weeks from completing her second year. We asked her to please finish out the year and then leave. At least she would have two years completed of college. But little did we know that she had not only failed her first year but was also failing her second year. She was running away from her problems, and she could not bear to tell us the truth. We had to let her go. We made sure she understood, though, that her decision would eliminate any future support to go back to school. In hindsight, her situation was desperate for her … and she left. As parents, we were frustrated and extremely concerned. (Ray Smith)

It wasn't just about me moving to Florida; it was about me cutting myself off from my parents, their money, and dropping out of school. I needed to go find myself, and I needed to do it on my own. At least, that was what I was trying to convince myself of. I wanted a whole new set of friends who would love and accept me, and there was a whole new pool of men who would increase my chances of finding true love.

I quit my job, sold some of my possessions, and moved to Florida with $30 in my pocket. I was excited for a whole new change and to get my life in order. I was in control now, not my parents, and I would be responsible for my own decisions. Little did I know that I was going to go down a path darker than anything else I had known in the last couple of years. I was Alice, and I fell into the rabbit hole where I just continued to fall. The light at the top of the rabbit hole got smaller and smaller until I finally hit rock bottom, and my efforts to stand back up while in pure darkness would be the hardest thing I would ever do.

> It (the human spirit) had turned from God and become its own idol, so that though it could still turn back to God, it could do so only by painful effort, and its inclination was self-ward. Hence pride and ambition, the desire to be lovely in its own eyes and to depress and humiliate all rivals, envy, and restless search for more, and still more, security, were now the attitudes that came easiest to it…. A new species, never made by God, had sinned itself into existence. (C. S. Lewis)

Chapter 3
THE LOST DAUGHTER

He also said: A man had two sons. The younger of them said to his father, "Father, give me the share of the estate I have coming to me." So, he distributed the assets to them. Not many days later, the younger son gathered together all he had and traveled to a distant country, where he squandered his estate in foolish living. After he had spent everything, a severe famine struck that country, and he had nothing. Then he went to work for one of the citizens of that country, who sent him into his fields to feed pigs. He longed to eat his fill from the carob pods the pigs were eating, but no one would give him any. When he came to his senses, he said, "How many of my father's hired hands have more than enough food, and here I am dying of hunger!"

—Luke 15:11–17

The story of the prodigal son is a famous tale that many of us can relate to in some way. Our self-centered nature can take over and drive us down paths of destruction that bring us to our knees. The problem is, often we don't realize we're on a destructive path until it's too late. We look back and try to figure out how we ended up in that place in our lives. Just like the prodigal son, making one bad decision after another, I was the lost daughter who didn't want or need any help. I was determined to live life to the fullest, so I did, right into the depths of darkness—a deep void filled with crack and cocaine.

Who knew that the girl who grew up in a Christian home with strong moral values would end up nearly destroying her life? This girl went from being a star athlete in high school to wild drinking and drug use in college, eventually ending up in a crack house in Florida. Yet God knew, and I now understand that He allowed me to endure those hard times so that He could use me. God was going to turn my situation into something good. Looking back on my time in Florida, I know without a doubt that God had His hand upon me through every moment. He wouldn't let me plunge completely down a path from which I couldn't return.

The first night in Florida was exciting—a new place, new friends, and most of all, new love prospects. I immediately started dating someone, only to discover that he occasionally indulged in smoking crack and snorting cocaine. Wanting to be the cool girlfriend, I followed suit. How I made the jump from drinking too much to smoking crack for the first time is somewhat of a mystery to me. It happened so fast. But God had a plan for me; I just wouldn't know it for a few years. They say hindsight is twenty-twenty, and believe me, I can vouch for that truth.

God's hand was and is in every situation I put myself in. I made choices that make me cringe in hindsight at the thought of God's reaction. I was completely turning away from Him, and I can only imagine the hurt and disappointment as He turned me over to the desires of my hardened heart. Yet He spared me death, jail, and so many other scenarios that could have been even worse. He showed me unconditional love even when I tried so hard not to acknowledge Him. Florida ended up being my tornado state—a time in my life when I was spinning in circles, causing destruction to my family, friends, and myself.

I lived with my cousin for a while then eventually started dating someone else and moved in with him, continuing my downfall. Nights of drinking on the patio with friends in the same complex were common. I had a pretty steady job working at a salon, which sparked my interest in attending cosmetology school, so I decided to enroll. Things appeared to be going well. I had a man I loved, an apartment, friends, and a good job. I was rebuilding my life, until my boyfriend stopped paying attention to me. The love I needed wasn't being fulfilled anymore, and I started to sink into a more depressive state.

I found myself trying everything I could to make him continue to love me. We soon ended things, he moved out, and I was alone again. I eventually started partying more at the bars and ended up deep back into drugs. Instead of doing cocaine maybe once every other week, I was doing it once a week, then twice a week, then almost every day of the week. You see, I still needed that void filled. The void that I thought would be filled by the love and attention of a man. When I did not have it or felt it was not enough, I tried to numb myself to take away the deep hurt.

God wired us to love and to be relational. But the relationship He designed is the relationship that we need to have with Him. If we do not have that relationship with Him, then we have a void in our hearts, and we start longing and searching for that one thing to fill it. The problem is no one can fill it except for Jesus Christ. If we ignore Him, we will continue to search to fill that void with things of this world. The void that is made for love and acceptance through Christ will never be filled by friends, family, a significant other, drugs, alcohol, and anything else that we use in this world. Yet we continue to search for that next thing that is going to make us happy. And when the temporary feeling of happiness wears off, we go out and look for that next best thing. It's a constant chase of contentment.

Throughout the first year in Florida, I made a lot of friends. I now recognize them more as acquaintances. My desire to continually find that happiness was almost without a conscience. If friends needed me for something but it interrupted my plans to party, I would blow them off so that I could go do what was on my agenda. Human tendency is to want as many friends as possible. It helps make us feel like we mean something in this world. But we also must know how to be a true friend to keep those relationships. I was not that friend. I wanted everyone to be there for me, but I was so self-centered that I did not return to the friendship.

One night, a friend's brother was in a car accident and was killed. I had just hung out with him a few weeks prior to the accident, so it was someone I knew. Everyone was getting ready to go over to the family's house to be with the family and express their condolences, but I had plans to go to a bar. So instead of canceling my plans to be a support for my friends, I simply said I was sorry for their loss and went to the bar.

I was so preoccupied with my own selfish wants that I didn't even stop and be that supportive friend. I had no idea how to be a friend, and I got called out on it. My friend, who is the sister of the man who died, said she didn't want anyone at the funeral who could care less that he died and asked that I not attend. So as everyone was getting ready to go to the funeral, I sat crying on my couch with this guilt of knowing what I did wrong. How could I be so selfish? It wasn't like I had something important that I couldn't cancel. I went to the bar! Really? This type of behavior was quickly turning me into someone I did not want to be or was not raised to be. It was the path of destruction that followed a pursuit of false happiness.

When you become addicted to drugs, love, and acceptance, life becomes all about you and not about anyone else. The god of self-interest starts to rear its ugly head, and the addictions form a heart of idolatry. It's unfortunate that it leaves a path of destruction and a feeling of not being complete or good enough or worthy enough of a life on this earth. What better way to self-protect than rationalize that no one else matters except you. You are the only one who is going to make things better for you. No one else is going to help with that, so follow your wants and needs, and take control of your life. It doesn't matter whom you step on because they don't matter. You are the one who matters. Right? As I would ultimately find out, I was so very, very wrong!

I started skipping out on work on a regular basis. I didn't care that I was leaving my employer high and dry. I made up excuse after excuse because I was either coming down from a high or I was on one of my cocaine binges. I would disappear for days at a time, not caring who might be wondering about me. I would tell myself that I had already broken all the relationships that I had, so it didn't matter. The relationships that I was building were all based on drugs and sex. That was becoming the determining factor of my value and self-worth. Every time I was disappointed with a relationship not working, more of my value would diminish—until I felt almost worthless.

My health started to go downhill very quickly. Not only was I severely depressed, but I wasn't eating. When you are snorting cocaine 24-7, you don't have much of an appetite. My diet consisted of drugs and alcohol and the occasional McDonald's dollar-menu cheeseburger (when I could round up enough change from the couch cushions). I became stick thin. My ribs started to show. I had no energy, no motivation, and no nutrition in my body, but I kept putting one foot in front of the other. I was determined to live my life my way, to find my one true love. And if I couldn't find him, then I would die trying.

I remember one weekend when my friend came into some money, and we had an inconceivable amount of cocaine. He wanted to share it with his friends, so we went on a three-day binge, partying like there was no tomorrow. I remember my heart rate racing throughout this time, and while talking to someone I just met, my nose started to bleed. God had his hand on me that weekend because I should have easily overdosed and died. I still can't believe that my whole thought process was trying to become that cool kid and be accepted among the popular crowd. How did I ever come to believe that people who constantly did drugs and partied were the cool kids? My identity was wrapped up in thinking there was value in being the one person whom people wanted to hang out with all the time. And I honestly believed that would only happen by being seen as the one who was up for anything.

There are many different stories I could tell you, but they all echo the same scenario. I went out; met people; did drugs; got drunk; slept with different men, thinking they would love me if I gave them what they wanted; and woke up the next morning depressed over what I did the night before. Then, I would start the same cycle again so I wouldn't feel the shame, guilt, and pain of my past behavior.

After two and a half years in Florida, I really had nothing to show for it. I reached the point where I could not handle my life anymore and had serious thoughts that no one would miss me if I was gone. I was having suicidal thoughts. But I don't remember ever seriously thinking about killing myself. By that, I mean that I didn't get to the planning stages of doing it. I really didn't even think much of how I would do it. It was more like Satan was trying to get me to that point. Pouncing on my fragile state and knowing that if he kept pecking at my thoughts of me being nothing, then he could really cause some serious damage.

Our thoughts can be one of the most dangerous weapons to ourselves and to others. Metaphorically speaking, it starts with one little thought that can spiral down, ending up in a pool of blood. Here is how it works. It starts with remembering what you did last night then thinking that you are a horrible person for doing what you did.

This evolves into full-blown guilt and shame, further exacerbated by recognizing that you have done this more than once, which only highlights even more that despicable person inside. How can anyone love you? You are never going to be able to get past your mistakes. No one will love you now if they know or find out what you have done. This begs the question, why are you even here? If you are not here, then no one will miss you because you are so horrible. No one will forgive you anyway. You end up making one of two choices. You go deeper into your suicidal thoughts, or you go back out to the bar or the liquor store to start washing away those painful feelings and trying to forget the memories that are swimming around in your head.

In this state, we almost always think there are only two options. But I can tell you from experience that there is a third option—and that is falling on your knees and crying out to God to make the bleeding stop. God will show himself to you if you ask Him and if you seek Him. He will orchestrate circumstances that will show himself to you in a way that really shakes you up. His design is to move you to an opportunity to cry out and seek Him. One night when I thought God knew

I was about to go past the point of no return, He spoke to me. He has his unique way of speaking with each of us and often in such a personal way that it touches the heart down to the core. For me, He spoke through a song, a song that would forever change my life.

I can still see it in my mind. I was sitting in my apartment on the floor, with my back leaning up against the stark white wall in my little dining area. I couldn't afford an actual table, so it was just an empty space. I had my CD player out on the floor, and I was listening to music and singing at the top of my lungs.

I have had these moments throughout my life when, even as a child, I would get into these emotional states, and the only thing I could do to control overwhelming emotions was to sing. I had a passion for singing. My family is probably visualizing this and laughing. It's okay to laugh and smile now, my dear family, but little did you know that sometimes it wasn't just about me wanting attention from singing; it was from overwhelming feelings of depression or loneliness. It was my release.

I was sitting on the floor with my legs out in front of me and singing, and there it was, a song that I had heard several times before. But it spoke loud and clear to me at that very moment. It was a song called "Tourniquet" by Evanescence. I listened to these words over and over for several hours that night. The synopsis of the song is talking about if it's too late to be saved and asking God to be a tourniquet to stop the bleeding. It's asking God to return our salvation. I highly suggest you Google the full lyrics and let them resonate with you.

When you're in such a dark place, it's hard to see any sort of light at the end of the tunnel. You just see darkness that tends to keep getting darker. But God opened my ears to the words of this song, and it got my attention. It didn't matter how worthless I felt. It didn't matter how much I felt hated and unloved. It didn't matter how much I had messed up in the past, because it is never too late. We are never too lost to cry out to God and ask for His forgiveness and for Him to be our tourniquet. God can stop the bleeding; we just must believe that He can.

I love the part of the song where it says this:

> My wounds cry for the grave, my soul cries for deliverance,
> Will I be denied Christ … Tourniquet. My suicide.

When we cry out to God from that dark, ugly place, our hearts are full of confusion and questions. Physically and mentally, we feel like dying, but our soul, the soul that God designed for us, cries out for healing. I have come to learn that the healing we need is God's unconditional love.

When the song said "Tourniquet … my suicide," I took that as a metaphor. For when we truly believe that God can heal us, then He is our tourniquet. My suicide was when I made the decision to stop my old ways. The moment I decided to try and turn my life around, I consciously laid my old self to rest and became a new person. My suicide. Never did I think that those two words would have a positive effect on me, but they did.

After listening to this song over and over, it became clear to me that I wanted a different life. I wanted it desperately. I had always believed in God but never had that personal relationship with Him. He was always something in the distance that I had little knowledge of in my head. He was never real and personal to me. I wish I could say that I accepted Him in my life and fully surrendered to Him that night, but I didn't. What I did do was cry out to Him, and in that moment, He gave me the strength to call my parents. I cried to them, asking for them to bring me home. After lots of prayer on their side, they decided to help bring me home. Unfortunately, I had a lot of medical issues that needed attention, including multiple exploratory surgeries to figure out why I was in a lot of pain, so I wasn't able to go home right away. It took another month or so for me to get that taken care of and for my parents to plan to get me home.

> Courtney had called us asking to come home. We prayed about it as we had been doing all along. We prayed for discernment and strength. We had decided when she left … to practice tough love with her. The most difficult times as parents were during these times of tough love. Is it time to help her? Is it too soon? Would we only continue to enable her? Has she learned and matured? A parent's natural inclination and instinct is to run and rescue their children, to protect them. But we knew there was greater love in helping them to suffer the consequences of their own decisions and to stand on their own feet. But … was it time to step back in and help? Although we did not know the depth of what she had experienced, we felt led to bring her home. She had asked, no, begged us, a number of times, to help her and we had said no. Something was different this time. We let her come home. (Ray Smith)

During that month, however, I reverted to my old ways. It only took a few days after God gave me that momentary clarity for me to slip back into darkness. The last month was quite a blur, and to this day, I can't remember everything that happened. It was as if I knew that my life would change drastically once I was back with my parents. I needed to get everything out before then. We all have our ups and downs, but it is a process. A process of having those God moments of clarity and seeking Him to Satan using our vulnerability and fragile state to bring us right back down. I went through three different surgeries that month to find out that I had a hernia hidden under my bladder, yet I would do drugs and drink until right before my surgeries. I was a mess.

My brother flew out to Florida so that he could help drive all my stuff back, and I was snorting the last of my coke in the bathroom as he was resting on the couch before we hit the road. That is how out of my mind I was. Part of me was screaming for me to be rescued, and the other part of me was screaming for me to continue this path to my death.

A war was waging in me, but God won the first battle. He got my attention that night a month ago, and although it was a short time, He saved me by putting things in motion. He saved me by giving me the strength to reach out to my family even though I was full of shame and embarrassment that I couldn't make it on my own. He saved me when I followed through with the decision to pack up my things in my truck and head out of Florida with my brother. The emotions that I had that day were so out of control it felt like I was in the middle of a hurricane out in the ocean. But I wasn't in a boat. It felt as if I had been thrown overboard and, although desperately trying to stay afloat, I was drowning. I was terrified.

The last five years of my life had been spent running down this desperate path to find love and acceptance through relationship after relationship and trying to see how many friends I could acquire. The more friends I had, the more I felt my heart filled. For five years, I had the independence of making my own decisions and doing what I wanted and when I wanted. Now I was going back home to live with my parents again. Back to rules, back to being watched, and back to what I thought was trying to be someone I wasn't, so I didn't disappoint them. Back to a family that I felt deep in my heart did not understand me or could learn to understand me. I was the black sheep.

> Her mother and I, on our end, did not know what to expect with Courtney. We had outlined the rules for her return. She must immediately look for and get a job. She had limited time to find an apartment to be on her own again. She had agreed to these terms. But we were also relieved at her returning home and planned to welcome her with open arms and be as supportive as we could. But we, too, were scared and relying on God's wisdom. (Ray Smith)

They did not know everything I had been through. They did not know the emotional wreck that would soon land on their doorstep. I felt I would not be able to relate to them, and they would not be able to relate to me. All these feelings of doubt and loneliness came rushing up inside me as I said goodbye to everything I had known for the last several years. I felt like I was going into the abyss of the unknown. I couldn't tell my parents about all the drugs I had been doing and all the mistakes I had made, because they would be so ashamed of me.

Not only did I have the emotional battle going on in me, but I was also having a physical battle going on as well. I was doing drugs almost seven days a week, and when you wreak that much havoc on your body, it starts to depend on that havoc. I had just had my final surgery a week before I left, so I had pain pills to help with the withdrawals, but I eventually ran out of those, as well. I honestly thought it would be so easy for me to just stop doing drugs. But I would cry myself to sleep a lot of the times in that first month I was home. I was trying not to show how much I was struggling, not only physically, but also mentally. It was a much harder task than I originally thought. But I had made the decision to change my life, so I was going to stuff everything down and put one foot in front of the other and continue forward, leaving my old self behind. I was essentially white knuckling it since I hadn't completely surrendered to God at this point.

Right when you start to make the tough decisions that are best for you, little things start to happen to knock you down. My brother and I were halfway through Texas on our way home, and a highway patrolman was going the opposite way. He decided he wanted to pull us over, and so he literally turned around and cut across the highway. As my brother rolled down his window, the patrolman immediately said he smelled marijuana and ordered both of us to step out of the vehicle so he could search it. Really? Here I was, trying to do the right thing with my life, and here we were, being pulled out of the vehicle. I had finally made it out of Florida, where I should have been arrested several times over, yet here I was, in the middle of nowhere in Texas, and I might be going to jail.

My brother looked at me with that question in his eyes of "What do you have in here?" I had all my belongings in boxes in the bed of the truck and no drugs on me whatsoever. I did, however, loan my truck to a friend who used it the week before I left. The officer separated my brother and me and searched the entire truck, including a thorough search of all the boxes I had in the back. We sat there for at least an hour or two in the hot sun, our hearts pounding out of our chests, wondering what was going to happen. My friend, apparently, had dropped a small bud of marijuana on the floorboard, and that was all the officer found, so after a stern lecture, he let us go.

It just goes to show that there are no guarantees that going in the right direction means a smooth path. Life is still going to challenge you in different ways. It is not always fair, and I guess that is why some people go off the rails in the first place. God protected me yet again even when I didn't deserve it. God will continually forgive us as we ask for it, but we will always have to deal with the consequences of our actions, which won't kill us but will only make us stronger. These experiences cause us to grow into who we are and into an identity grounded in Christ.

So just like the prodigal son, I left to venture out on my own, and I found myself squandering all my money, my morals, and everything my parents had taught me growing up. But I eventually made it back home. So as the story of the prodigal son continues, the story of the lost daughter continues, as well.

> "I will set out and go back to my father and say to him: Father, I have sinned against heaven and against you. I am no longer worthy to be called your son; make me like one of your hired servants." So, he got up and went to his father. But while he was still a long way off, his father saw him and was filled with compassion for him; he ran to his son, threw his arms around him, and kissed him. (Luke 15:18–21)

I made it to Southern California, where my parents were now living, and although there was a lot of work to be done to repair my relationship with them, they forgave me, opened their arms, and let me run home to them with hearts full of love. God saved me again by giving God-fearing parents who prayed to know when to help me and bring me home. Now it was time for me to put on my big-girl pants and start to rebuild my life into a life that could make my family proud, a life that could ultimately make me proud. Little did I know that I would come to learn that it wasn't about making either one of us proud, but it was about making our Sovereign Lord proud.

Chapter 4
TRANSITION

Times of transitions are strenuous, but I love them. They are an opportunity to purge, rethink priorities, and be intentional about new habits. We can make our new normal anything we want.

—Kristin Armstrong

Transitions can be difficult as you let go of one chapter of your life and start the next. It can be even more challenging when you're finishing an entire book and trying to rewrite a second novel, but I was determined. I was done being poor and a disappointment not only to my family, but more importantly, to myself. I started on the path to healing and, hopefully, creating some measure of success.

Coming home was difficult. I was a complete emotional wreck. But I poured all that emotional energy into finding a job. Within the first couple of weeks, I found what is called a temp-to-hire job as an accounting clerk at a mortgage company. I really was just looking for a job, any job, so that I could begin to get back on my feet. But to my surprise and delight, I quickly found that I really enjoyed accounting. I had always been good at math, and I have always had a lot of varied interests growing up, especially when it came to playtime.

Normal girls like to play with Barbies, but me? No, I liked to play office. My uncle, who worked for himself, used to let my brothers, sister, and me raid his supply closet when we went to visit, and I would have pads of paper, pens, calculators, the works. I would set up my little station and pretend that I had a very important office job. I guess I should have known that accounting would be right up my alley.

I started off with a basic job and really was only focused on getting stabilized and starting to prove to myself and others that I was responsible. That what I had left in Florida was going to be just a bad dream someday. I was scared. My confidence as to who I was and what I should be doing or not doing had taken a terrible beating. My self-confidence and self-esteem were in the toilet. And I wasn't just scared; I was also embarrassed. A deep-down, agonizing kind of embarrassment. You know how every family has a "black sheep"? Well, I felt that was how the family viewed me. I felt like I was a colossal failure on so many fronts, and I really wasn't sure if I would have the strength and stamina to get it all back together. And I desperately did not want to disappoint my family again.

Despite my fears, I put one foot in front of the other, and on a daily basis, I did my best to settle into my new job. I was determined to make something work. The discovery of an affinity and delight in accounting was a godsend. It had an excitement to it. Until then, I had never really felt like I knew what I enjoyed and/or might be good at. It was a boost to my self-esteem that I could have some value, even in something as simple as being good at numbers. I vividly remember going home and excitedly telling my dad about how I thought I had found something that I really enjoyed and was good at. I think he was excited for me, as well, but in a cautious sort of way. I can't say that I really blamed him; after all, my track record up to that point had not really been stellar. Okay, it had been a real mess. But I knew that he and my mom supported me in every way.

Over time, I successfully settled into my job and received lots of affirmation from my bosses. The longer I was there, the more confident I became. I also realized that my love for accounting and numbers did not fade away; it only solidified my desire to pursue it as a career. However, there was just one problem—I did not have a degree in accounting. I could see that if I wanted to advance in the field, I would have to consider going back to school. That thought terrified me, driven by my lack of confidence. I really doubted if I would have the discipline to get through school.

My first attempt at it (before I dropped out to go to Florida) ended in failure, which reinforced my doubts and fears. I was afraid of starting something like that again and failing once more. I just didn't want my family and friends to witness that disappointment again. I didn't think I could emotionally handle the stress of it.

Despite my fears, I approached my dad and discussed the idea of going back to school. I wasn't sure how he would react, so I was apprehensive about it. I also remembered that he had made it clear to me when I dropped out of college that he wouldn't pay for it if I decided to go back again. That had been his rule for all of us kids—he would cover the first four years out of high school and nothing more. If we didn't finish by then, it was on us. I didn't want him to think I was asking for a handout. This was something I needed to do if I was going to do it. I needed to prove something to myself and, I think, to everyone, really.

My conversation with my dad went very well. He was very encouraging and talked about taking one class at a time, easing back into a pattern and routine. He kept talking about a bachelor's degree, but I kept telling him that I couldn't even think about that. I had to focus on getting an AA (at most) for now, and I wasn't even sure if I could handle that. I was very scared of the whole process. My confidence was still very low, and the memories of failing in San Diego and Florida were still fresh. But I decided to just start somewhere and see what happened.

I started going back to school for accounting. I decided to start small and found an online associate degree program. As I progressed through the first few classes, I remember my dad telling me to just keep going and not get discouraged. He assured me that soon, taking classes would become a regular, routine part of my schedule and that, by the time I turned thirty or thirty-one, I could have my master's degree. He had already been calculating each program and how long it would take me to finish. All I could think of was how overwhelming that sounded. Baby steps were all I was prepared to take. Let me just finish my AA. I had no idea how far I would go, but my dad did.

Just as he had said, the next thing I knew, I had completed my AA. I thought, *That wasn't so bad*, and decided to continue, aiming for my bachelor's degree in accounting. The next thing I knew, I had my degree. The funny thing is that as I achieved each little milestone, my confidence grew. By the time I turned thirty-one, I had not only earned my AA and bachelor's degrees in accounting, but also obtained my MBA degree with an emphasis in accounting. A lot of hard work went into working full-time and going to school full-time, but I did it. I even have student loans to prove it.

Some people think there is no way they can work and go to school, but I am here to tell you that anything is possible if you put your mind to it. Put one foot in front of the other. It is a lot of sacrifice on your free time, but it's a temporary situation. Once you graduate, not only do you get some of your free time back, but you have accomplished something great. Not everyone has the determination to finish higher education, but when you do, it's the most rewarding feeling. And as my dad often said during this process, once you get the degree, no one can ever take it from you. You will have it for your benefit for the rest of your life. Make the short-term sacrifice for the long-term gain.

My career was everything to me during and after my school years. That was my main and sometimes sole focus for the next few years, working and impressing people and moving up in the corporate world. My motto was work hard then play hard. I would go out on the weekends and drink until I was passed out or throwing up all night, all in the name of having a good time. I was still going from one relationship to another, trying to find that perfect love. Lo and behold, I found myself with the same problem that I had in Florida, excluding the drugs. I was back on track with work and school, but I was still longing for that love and acceptance and still searching for it in all the wrong places.

It just goes to show you that you can't run from the underlying problem of why you decide to do drugs or drink excessively. It will follow you no matter where you go unless you meet the problem head-on. Changing locations or starting something new only masks the underlying emotional insecurities and needs. The decision needs to be made, whether to make fresh, new starts over and over versus whether you want complete healing and complete freedom. It was clear that I needed to make a decision. It was a dead end. I had tried all the things that I thought would make it better and/or satisfy the longing, loneliness, and emptiness in my heart. I desperately wanted healing and freedom, but the question was, how do I get that healing and freedom?

I found out later that I wanted complete freedom, but the only way I was going to get that was through Jesus Christ and fully surrendering my life to Him. As the quote at the beginning of the chapter said, we get to make it anything we want. We must choose. It is our decision to grasp onto the transition of this world or the transformation that Jesus Christ can give us.

The key words to a full transformation are *full surrender*. I knew in my head that I needed to get back into church. It was the right thing to do, but my heart was not fully surrendered. You see, we all have this little issue called control. We always want to hold on to everything that is happening in our lives and the people around us because we feel that we can make the right decisions. Even when we do give our lives fully to Christ, we give up our burdens and control to those burdens, laying them at Christ's feet. Then when the timing is not what we think it should be or how the problem should be solved, then we take it back, and it goes back and forth.

I had a hard time with the concept of me not being in charge of my life and trusting someone I could not see or physically touch. How could I trust someone that I have not spent time with and shaken their hands? How can I not worry about situations that are happening that are directly affecting me and trust that God knew best? I just couldn't get over it, but I continued to go to church, and I started to get heavily involved with the church through the kids' program. I figured if I kept going and doing what was right, then everything would eventually fall into place. I found out how wrong I could be.

During transitions, Satan will try to knock you back down if you show the slightest interest in a relationship with Christ, and that is what Satan did. He took a vulnerable spot in me and turned me upside down. He turned my view of the church into a very bitter taste. After being heavily involved in the church I was attending at that time, I ended up having to have another surgery. This time I had complications and was out of commission for about three months. Not one person from the church or the team that I volunteered with called me to see how I was doing after the surgery or even cared enough to see why I hadn't returned to church shortly after my surgery.

I always remembered the pastor talking about involving yourself in the church so that you can become part of the church family. He said if you go to church every Sunday and then bolt without becoming involved, then you can't expect to feel part of the community and family that a church body provides. Well, I got involved. I was part of three weekend services a month, volunteering the whole weekend, and I didn't even get a call after my surgery. A bitter taste was left in my mouth.

So naturally, my thoughts went to "Why am I killing myself trying to go to church and do what I am supposed to be doing if no one cares about me? The church is supposed to take care of each other and to love and support one another. Where was the love? Where was the support?" I was crushed. My heart said, "Forget them," and I stopped going to church altogether and turned off my heart to this whole church and God thing. I tried, right? It just didn't work out. It was not for me. I was doing just fine in my life. I had a great job. I was on track with school. I had a bunch of friends. I was doing just fine.

I continued this path of "me, myself, and I," and Satan capitalized on it. Have you ever felt that you are doing great in what you are doing, and you are proud of yourself for everything you did? You did it. Sure, you might have had help, but you picked yourself up off the ground when times were low. You got a new job and career. You enrolled yourself in school. You could pay your own bills and not worry about it. You had great friendships that you maintained. Get my point of "you, you, you" or "I, I, I." That is how I felt. I was comfortable in my life; everything was going smoothly, and life was great.

I will never forget watching *God's Not Dead*, and Dean Cain's character was sitting with his mother, who had Alzheimer's. He was sitting there full of arrogance and not wanting to be there. He was too good to be somewhere where no one would know he was there. Until God spoke through her. She said that sometimes, Satan will give us great lives so that we don't know that we are living in a prison cell until it's too late. If our lives are great and we are comfortable, then how are we to know that something is wrong? That we really need Jesus to complete us? This hit home to me when I saw that, because that was me for so long, thinking I was doing just fine on my own, so why search out faith? That just seemed ridiculous to me.

It wasn't until a few years later that I started to feel that I was truly missing something that I could not fill. I had an emptiness to me that I didn't quite understand. It didn't matter what I did to try and fill that void; nothing would work. My mom started inviting me to the women's luncheons at her church and introducing me to ladies, and that was okay. She invited me to one of her women's retreats with her church, and I was, let's say, uncomfortable the whole time, but I was doing it for her. God had a different idea. My heart wasn't quite in the right place, but God used my mom to slowly start planting seeds in me. I might have been uncomfortable going to the retreat, but God was slowly starting to open my heart to the idea of possibly going back to church, even though there were doubts. Doubts of believing in something you couldn't see face-to-face as you and I would see each other sitting across the dinner table.

Chapter 5
INTANGIBLE GOD

If you hold to my teaching, you are really my disciples.
Then you will know the truth, and the truth will
set you free.

—John 8:31–32

My journey thus far had been a path of separation from God, marked by my habitual sins, negative experiences with church, and doubts. Numerous questions lingered, but my primary inquiry centered on grappling with the concept of believing in an intangible God amid the tangible world. It felt surreal and bewildering to invest faith in something beyond sight, touch, or feeling. Not only was I expected to believe in this God but was also urged to relinquish control over my life. Yet I hesitated, unsure if I was prepared to surrender, even if my life veered off my planned course.

In today's society, yielding to selfish desires has become commonplace. Advertisements often promote products with promises of self-fulfillment upon purchase. Sexual imagery saturates billboards, TV shows, movies, and commercials, making uncomfortable moments like watching a Viagra commercial with family routine. Whatever happened to modesty, where intimacy remained private, confined to marital relationships? Nowadays, abstaining from premarital sex or cohabitation garners scrutiny. Alcohol is glorified as the panacea for stress and pressure, depicted in media as the go-to solution for troubled characters. Our culture glorifies selfish indulgence, blinding many to the underlying evil.

My greatest apprehension about embracing Christ fully was anticipating my friends' reactions to the changes I'd undergo. Fear of losing their acceptance overshadowed the potential blessings awaiting me. This fear, compounded by familial inquiries, fueled my reluctance. The pressure to conform only pushed me further away. No one would dictate when or if I should accept Christ.

Then, there was the ultimate concern: What would people think of me? I dreaded being labeled a "Jesus freak" for believing in seemingly implausible miracles—Noah's flood, the miraculous feeding of thousands, and resurrection stories. The age-old question haunted me: If God is love, why does He permit suffering?

Have you ever heard the phrase "Perception is reality"? This phrase basically means that our perception of something, absent contrary facts, creates the reality in which we live, see the world, and make decisions. It contributes heavily to our worldview.

It is important to realize that our perception may become our reality, but that doesn't mean it is an accurate, truthful view of life. For example, all these questions are asked, and then God's answers are dismissed as if it's just not possible. Not only can we not really believe in an intangible God with all His miracles, but we will also not submit ourselves to an authority that we can't see, feel, or touch. We will not surrender to a God who is inconsistent in how He treats people. See how that works?

That perception is wrong, and it is not truth. We have been living in a world that is full of wrong perceptions perpetrated by a secular worldview that does everything it can to separate us from the truth of God and our purpose here on this earth.

Let me tell you a little story, a story that has been told many times at the dinner table just to reminisce and to laugh. It was the beginning of summer in Tracy, California. It was the time when summer was beginning, and it started to get hot. Northern California has a dry heat that cracks your skin and chaps your lips. It turns much of the vegetation brown instead of green, and it was not uncommon to see a large piece of tumbleweed rolling down or across the streets. My family and I lived in a house at the end of a cul-de-sac, and it was right before we decided to put in an in-ground pool. In the far corner of the yard was a large patch of dry weeds three to four feet tall.

Now, picture it: it was a Saturday morning, and all of us kids were sitting watching the morning cartoons. My dad opened the sliding glass door from the backyard and yelled, "Hey kids!! Want to see something really cool?" Of course, all four of us charged out the back sliding glass door and followed my dad. Who doesn't want to see something cool, right? He brought us over to the corner of the yard and said to look over there and pointed to a place just inside the weeds. "What is it, Dad?" one of us said, and he said, "Look closely, it's a snake! Do you see it?"

We all got a little closer and leaned in a little bit, and we saw it. Right there in the middle of the weeds was a snake that seemed to be four feet long and was just lying there. The snake was probably more like one foot, but you know how we all exaggerate when telling stories.

My dad then said, "I'm going to grab it." My mom came out and chimed in, "Honey, don't you dare. We don't know if it is poisonous or not. We should just call animal rescue." All our hearts were beating out of our chests. We did not want our dad to get hurt if the snake bit him, but secretly, we were thinking that this was way cool.

After some back-and-forth between my parents, my dad decided to go for it. He slowly reached in and then quickly grabbed the snake and lifted it out of the grass. The snake started squirming in his hands, and my dad had his hands up, trying to get a better grip on the snake. All four of our eyes immediately opened wide, and we all scattered in four different directions. My brother and I started running to the back sliding glass door, while my sister ran off to the other side of the house, and my youngest brother ran off in another direction.

My brother got to the sliding glass door just a couple of seconds before I did. You would think that being a loving younger brother, he would hold the sliding glass door open for me, but he did not. He slammed it shut and then locked the door so I couldn't get in. Typical brother behavior. I slammed against the door, turned around, and realized I had no place to go. My dad was coming my way with the snake in his hands, and my brother had locked me out of the house.

I was paralyzed with fear. My heart was beating wildly, and I was scared to death. My dad got up really close, and I started to slide down the sliding glass door all the way to the ground, as I screamed at the top of my lungs. I ended up in a seated position, trying to cover myself as if putting my hands over my head were going to save me from this monstrous, poisonous snake. My dad suddenly stopped, and I got the courage to look up. He was still holding the snake, and then he slowly put the snake's head in his mouth.

My brother's face as he looked out the sliding door went into a shocked look, and my eyes got really big. Then there was silence, no more screaming, just this shocked look on our faces. The snake was not real. My mom got the snake at a nature store, and my parents came up with this elaborate plan to trick us.

The point is that my perception was that the snake was real, and I reacted accordingly. My reality that morning was that I was going to die as my dad was chasing me with a poisonous snake. But that perception wasn't the truth. The truth was that the snake was fake and that really if I thought about it, I was pretty sure my dad would not try to kill me with a snake. I knew that my dad loved me very much. He would not let anything hurt me. Yet I forgot that in the panic of the moment.

Take a moment for that to set in. I wish it had set in with me as I was running for my life that day. I would have saved myself a lot of humiliation. But it has created a story that my family will forever remember and will be passed down from generation to generation.

If my perception at the time was that I saw being a Christian was more of a sacrifice than a blessing, was that the wrong perception? Were my reality and my knowledge at that time the truth? And if not, then what was the truth? If I found out what the truth was, would I still make the right decision? After all, I hadn't been quite so good in that department in my past.

Truth

My pastor once said that the most important thing we can do is to be willing to seek the truth and to ask God to show it to us. You may be one of those people who adamantly denies God and says you don't believe in Him. Or you may be like I was, with questions and doubts. Or maybe you are going to church to appease someone else, but without any intentions of falling for this whole "God thing." Wherever you may be, let me ask this question: Would you rather research and seek the truth to make sure that the decision you are making is accurate?

Take the concept of fully understanding all the Bible issues out of the equation. If you have truly decided that you do not want to follow Jesus, are you interested in really making sure that you have made an informed decision? God's only desire is for you to seek the truth. It doesn't mean you have to know all the answers, but seek the truth, and ask Him to show you that He really does exist. He will show you. He will guide you along a path to understand His truth. And you don't have to be a Bible scholar to get there.

Jesus said the truth will set you free.

> To the Jews who had believed him, Jesus said, "If you hold to my teaching, you are really my disciples. Then you will know the truth, and the truth will set you free." (John 8:31–32)

The truth is God's word. We live in a world where emotions are at the forefront and often solely used as a guide to how we live our lives. However, we should make decisions based not only on our knowledge but on our hearts, as well. But if our heart and mind are not aligned, then we will make the wrong decision. How often I made the wrong decision and denied myself the blessings that God wanted to give me because my mind was not in line with what my heart knew to be the truth. My pastor once said that the biggest jump you will ever take in life is only twelve inches from your head to your heart.

The truth will set us free, but we must seek it and be open to it. I made the decision too many times to deny living a life for Christ because, frankly, I didn't want to follow anyone else but myself. I wanted to be in control. Fully surrendering to someone is hard, but surrendering to what I thought was a mystical character is even harder. I was constantly searching for more in my life. I did not have that sense of peace and joy and love. God was knocking at my heart the whole time; I just needed to open my mind enough to hear him and give Him a chance to align my heart and my mind with his desires and his love.

The truth is that God is sovereign, and God is love. The Bible gives us a great description of who He is and of His character. We may not be able to see Him physically as if I can see someone right in front of me, but if we open ourselves to the truth, then we open ourselves up to changed hearts that will be able to see and experience Him in a whole new way. Sometimes we need to take a step and start reaching out for the truth even if our feelings are telling us differently. The more aligned our hearts and our minds become, the more we seek the truth, and the quicker our transformation will be.

The hardest thing about seeking God and understanding Him is the fact that we see so much pain and suffering in the world. If God is love, then how can He allow the pain and suffering to happen to so many good people? This is something that I couldn't grasp. Have you wondered the same thing? You have had so many questions that you want answered and especially the one that if God can prevent it, then why doesn't He? That doesn't seem like a very loving god. Why should we choose to follow a god who lets these things happen?

One answer is that we seem to focus only on the situations that just don't seem fair, just, or right. I believe that Satan uses this confusion to keep our hearts and minds misaligned. If we focused on all the good in the world and look for God's hand in that, it would be a different story. To be honest, we may never fully understand God's actions until we see Him in heaven.

But the truth is that God will always use every situation for good no matter what happens. Can He prevent something bad from happening? Absolutely, and I believe in many cases He does. We just don't see it all the time.

God's desire is for us to choose to love and follow Him through the free exercise of our own free will. If He were to force us to follow Him, then what type of relationship would that be? However, there is a risk in allowing people to decide for themselves what they believe. There will be those who choose to live a life separate from God and a life of sinful behavior.

By allowing the world to take its natural course, it often reaps terrible and painful consequences. I can't always say that I understand what God allows and doesn't allow. Many times, it appears that the pain and suffering far outweigh our human ability to understand what good can possibly come out of certain situations.

There are times when I see something happen and grieve with other people not only in their suffering but also in their confusion and cries to God as to why. Why did this have to happen? Why did this or that person have to suffer so much? I do get angry and at times find myself yelling at God in my lack of understanding. But I also have a conversation with Him, and at the end of the day, I must trust that God is in control.

One day, He will avenge those who have suffered by punishing the people who need to be punished. It is the realization that the ultimate thing that we live and hope for is living eternally in heaven with Christ. That one day, there will be no more tears and suffering. In the end, the good will outweigh the bad as we know Christ won when He died on the cross for our sins. The victory is His in the end.

I am old enough and experienced enough to know that God always uses bad things for good. We may not always see it right away, but He will use it for good. He allows us to go through different situations so that He can use us later to carry out His work and to help others.

God allowed me to go through different situations because He knew that I would one day be helping other women become free from their struggles. Had I not gone through different trials and tribulations throughout my life, I would not be able to help them in a way that would bring them closer to God because I would not be able to relate to them. I would not have an understanding that comes from a heart that has been there.

Another related question—or I should say statement—comes from an attitude of self-assessment in being a good person; the logic being that if I am a good person and God is this great and loving God, how could He not let me into heaven?

The biggest misconception in this world today is that people are inherently good. A good example of this is schools' self-esteem programs that emphasize that no matter what you do, you are a good person. The message is reinforced that people are born good. The truth is that this is an idea born out of the world we live in. It is not conducive to God's Word, which clearly states we are born into sin.

Sin is anything that separates us from a relationship with God. We naturally and often choose to separate ourselves because we are inherently selfish, born into sin. We want things our way and will work independently of God to obtain them.

I remember one day with my mom and my little brother in a department store. My brother was about two years old, and I was around nine at that time. I don't recall all the details, but my brother wanted something from my mom, and she said no. Whatever it was, he desired it so fervently that he believed throwing himself on the floor, crying and screaming, would make my mother give in. He was two, wanting what he wanted regardless of the means. Perhaps you've witnessed similar scenes in malls or stores, where a child's refusal leads to dramatic tactics, in hopes of changing the parent's mind.

Human nature tends toward selfishness and sin, evident from early ages, reinforcing the truth of God's Word that we are born into sin, not inherently good. As we grow older and comprehend, we have the choice, through our free will, to follow Christ.

God's grace is freely given, a gift to us. We don't earn salvation or forgiveness through good works. Jesus's sacrifice on the cross grants forgiveness to all who believe in Him, covering their sins—past, present, and future. We don't merit it, but we must make the conscious, willful choice to live for Christ.

> For God so loved the world that he gave his one and only Son, that whoever believes in him shall not perish but have eternal life. (John 3:16)

The gospel is simple; however, sometimes, we get in our own way and make it unnecessarily complex. That is in part because of our lack of understanding of the Almighty God in comparison to the small world in which we live. But because of God's incredible mercy and grace, just as I was starting to seek answers and open my heart to the possibility that God is the answer, He answered.

> Here I am! I stand at the door and knock. If anyone hears my voice and opens the door, I will come in and eat with that person, and they with me. (Revelation 3:20)

Chapter 6
RESCUED

Blessed are they whose transgressions are forgiven, whose
sins are covered. Blessed is the man whose sin the Lord
will never count against him.
—Romans 4:7–8

One of my favorite things to read about and watch is natural
disaster books and movies. There is something about the
intensity of the movie and the realization that these things can
really happen. My mom, knowing this, introduced me to the
works of author Joel Rosenberg, who has now become one of
my all-time favorite authors. He writes fiction and nonfiction
based on current world events, especially throughout the Middle
East. He ties these events to end-times biblical prophecy.

Sometimes, he does this with fiction; other books are
nonfiction, similar to a written documentary. His books are
fascinating to read, and within the first few minutes of reading
his first book, I was hooked. He writes with an intensity that is
so captivating that you can't put the book down. Reading about
the end-times and tying it in with modern culture was an eye-
opener that made me realize that we live in a precarious time
that is both frightening and exciting at the same time.

His books began to open my eyes. I have to be honest and say that I always thought that I could live my life the way I wanted, have all the fun and control, and then swoop in to accept Jesus right before the finish line. What was I ever thinking? I did not know when Jesus would come back, so I should have been always ready. I could not just wait until the end because it might be too late. As I read his books, my mind was spinning, and my heart was opening more and more to the idea of following Jesus. After I was done with his initial books, I started to read the Left Behind series.

I couldn't read enough about the Tribulation and the Rapture and everything that was happening currently, and then it happened. The moment arrived when God got my attention. The way God grabs our attention is unique to every individual. For one person, it may be a tragedy. For another person, it may be a family member dragging them to church, only to hear God speaking to their heart. My point is that everyone is different, and I most certainly am no exception. Well, maybe a bit unusual, because, you see, God used trumpets with me.

> Then the seven angels who had the seven trumpets prepared to sound them. (Revelation 8:6)

I always equated trumpets with Jesus coming back, especially in the mindset of reading about the Tribulation and the biblical prophecies that tie in with the end-times. What happened next was a jaw-dropping moment for me that truly changed the trajectory of my life.

I lived in a second-story apartment across the street from the Crystal Cathedral in Orange, California. It was a very well-known church for its architecture and services. I was sitting on my couch on a bright, sunny day. It was one of those days to open all the curtains and windows so you could feel the sunlight and crisp air coming through your apartment. I was very relaxed and content sitting on my couch, reclining my feet. I had the TV on in the background, and I was reading one of the books from the Left Behind series.

Suddenly, I heard the sound of trumpets. This was not just any normal sound of trumpets, but a trumpet sound that was loud enough to shake my apartment walls. I immediately jumped up, but I was all flailing arms and legs as I was trying to get up while trying to push down my recliner at the same time. I can only imagine how it must have looked. I was utterly panicked. I almost tripped over it because the recliner didn't close all the way. It popped right back up, hitting the back of my legs, but it didn't matter because I was in straight panic mode.

I started to breathe heavily, and my heart was pounding out of my chest. I literally thought I might be having a heart attack, and it was all due to the fact that I was thinking that the Rapture had occurred, and I had been left behind. That's right. I thought the trumpets blew and the Rapture had happened, and I was still there because I had resisted deciding to surrender my life to Christ.

I immediately called my mom. I knew that if she answered, then there was no way that the Rapture had happened. She is a true woman of God, and she would be one of the first people up there standing next to Jesus. Now, my mom is one of those people who do not always have her phone easily accessible. She normally has it at the bottom of her purse, or she forgot where she put it. As a result, she was taking a while to answer the phone.

Try and picture me completely out of sorts, while she is probably nonchalantly digging through her purse, trying to find her phone. It seemed like an eternity (pun intended) until she finally answered. Immediately, a weight lifted off my shoulders, one, quite frankly, that I didn't realize was there. I immediately said, "Good, you are still here!"

Of course, she had no idea what was going on, so I started to tell her while talking a mile a minute. As it dawned on her the circumstances and what I was thinking, all she could do was start to laugh. Now, in hindsight, I am laughing hysterically as I write about that experience. It is funny now, but I tell you the anxiety and the fear that I felt for that small moment was enough to scare the daylights out of me.

I no longer wanted to wait to truly accept Christ in full surrender; I did it right then and there. Granted, as you know, I accepted Christ when I was eleven from earlier in the book, but I did not fully surrender my life to Him, which is a tremendous difference. But this time, it truly was different. It was full and unconditional. I now made the decision for me, and not because I grew up in the church and it was the thing I had to do.

I no longer wanted to oversee my life. I had already made quite a mess of it. I needed someone who loved me unconditionally. I needed someone who knew what was going to be best for me even when I couldn't figure it out for myself. I needed someone who could forgive me for my past sins (and there was a lot to forgive) and to say it does not matter because you are my child, and I love you.

I needed God, and I finally found that "something" that would fill the emptiness in my heart. I was now complete. The one thing that I needed all those years, Jesus, had been standing right next to me every moment of every day, whispering in my ear that He was right there, and all I had to do was seek Him.

By the sound of trumpets, God got my attention, and He rescued me. The peace and joy that I felt were overwhelming. A dark mist had been hanging over my head, and as time went on, that dark mist kept getting darker and thicker, slowly starting to suffocate me. Part of me knew something was not right, but I could not quite put my finger on it, so the darkness overwhelmed me until Jesus rescued me.

When I made the decision to fully surrender myself to Christ, it was like that thick dark mist evaporated into thin air, and I could breathe again. I was breathing fresh, crisp mountain air with no toxic pollution, and I was on cloud nine.

My desire to follow Christ was on fire. I started going to church regularly and really listening to the sermons. But what was next? I didn't really know what was expected of me as a new child of God. I knew it wasn't enough to just go to church regularly, and I had so much to learn.

God was slowly starting to show me the areas of my life I needed to start changing. It wasn't just about learning more about Jesus; it was about making changes in my life and applying the knowledge that I was learning.

God will always reveal things that you need to work on. A special sermon will convict you in a certain way, or He will just lay something on your heart. For me, I was on fire for God but still trying to live my life in the way that I had always lived it. I had been in complete control of my life for so long that it was all I knew how to do. But that was the problem: I had lived my life independent of God. I didn't incorporate God into my life.

For so long, it had been all about me, so even though I was going to church and wanted to learn and was reading my Bible, I needed to change even more. The old activities that I used to do slowly began to lose their appeal. It just was not as much fun. God was convicting me and transforming my heart over time as I still indulged in my old life and friends.

Even though I had changed and committed my life to Christ, it is still hard to go cold turkey on your friends and old habits. But over time, I found out that going out and drinking excessively was not that much fun anymore. It was taking me longer to recover from the hangovers, and I found that it didn't have the same meaning for me that it used to have.

Going from one boyfriend to another and sleeping with them was not working out anymore. I found myself wanting to find a man who went to church and had the same values. The men that I used to date were not emotionally attractive to me anymore. God opened my eyes to how I should be treated from a biblical perspective and how I deserved to be treated as His child.

Intimacy was something special to be shared between a man and a woman within the confines and commitment of marriage. A few months after I fully surrendered my life, I made the decision to wait until I got married to experience that intimacy once again. I made the choice to change my outlook on dating and to completely revamp my idea of what I wanted in a man and a relationship.

This led me to transform how I dressed. God opened my heart to the idea of modesty. It was something that I had never really taken the time to look at or even seriously considered. In today's world, it is okay and encouraged to wear low-cut shirts that reveal cleavage and shorts where your butt is hanging out. The sexier, the better.

Your identity becomes wrapped up in how you look on the outside and always wanting to adapt to the trends of the materialistic society in which we live. For many years, I had no problem going along with this concept. But in my newfound commitment to Christ, I started to feel self-conscious. The clothing that I bought was still fashionable but covered more of my body.

It's amazing to look back to see how much God transformed my life in different areas. What I once thought was okay and normal was the opposite of what I now know to be right in the eyes of God. In my transformation, God completely changed my desires. I never thought I could change this much, but with God, anything is possible. Little by little, God showed me different things He wanted me to work on. I am a continuous work in progress.

Unfortunately, I don't always hear Him until He knocks the wind out of me or pulls the rug out from underneath me. A few years back, about a year after my decision to live for Christ, He did just that. God rescued me when I accepted Him into my life, but He rescued me again when He showed me what I really needed to work on: my past.

God had already forgiven me of my past sins, and I mean all my sins, but I have also come to believe that He wants us to learn from our past mistakes. So even though He has forgiven our sins and forgotten them, there is value at times to revisit our past to understand the whys of the choices and decisions made at that time. How else are we going to learn from it and grow?

I understand that it is desirable to acknowledge our past and then forget it. Many memories are painful and embarrassing. God wants to be able to use all bad things for good, so there is a process for Him to be able to use someone to do His work. We must know and understand that we are broken and why we were broken in order for God to start rebuilding us in His image and in His character. It's amazing how God gets my attention each time. Once, it was trumpets from the Crystal Cathedral, and now it was a major neck surgery.

For two years, I had been having neck pain and upper back spasms. There were times when I would wake up and not be able to lift my neck without shooting pains going down my left arm and the left side of my back. I was constantly getting headaches and in pain. At first, I thought it was related to working at a desk at work. I would sit in front of a computer all day, sometimes ten hours a day, and my poor posture did not help. I often went to the doctor to get prescriptions for Vicodin and muscle relaxers.

This would alleviate the flare-ups for a short time, only to just go through it again a month later. After approximately two years of this, I started to feel weakness in my left arm and tingling in my fingers. I told the doctor that I needed to be referred to a specialist. He agreed and prescribed an MRI and a visit to the Brain and Spine Institute. Within a minute of the doctor seeing my MRI, he diagnosed me with a degenerative bulging disc between my C5 and C6 cervical (neck) vertebrae.

He said it had been many years since he had encountered this level of trauma in someone under forty. I was thankful that something was actually wrong, and it wasn't just my imagination, but at the same time, I was scared to death that I now needed neck surgery. He wanted to get it done within the next three weeks.

Up to this point, I had been on pain medication for several weeks, so by the time of the surgery, I had been on pain medication for a total of six weeks. The surgery came and went, and I was in a lot of pain for the first four weeks after surgery. I was taking double the dose of pain medication every four to five hours so that I would not risk the pain getting too severe.

I pushed myself to be back at work in three weeks, but I would need to be in a neck brace for a total of six weeks.

After six weeks, I was to go through physical therapy to get the strength back in my neck and shoulder muscles. Everything was going according to plan until I was out of pain medication. I decided I didn't need it anymore, so I threw the bottle away. Within the first eight hours, I started to feel a little under the weather, and twenty-four hours later, I was going through physical withdrawals, although I did not recognize it at first.

I never wanted to think about withdrawal again, let alone have it be the worst withdrawal I had ever been through. Initially, I started to shake or tremble a little, and I couldn't focus. My head began pounding, and my whole body itched and, at times, felt like it was on fire. My stomach was in knots; my hands clammy; and food was not digesting properly.

The worst part was not being able to get warm. I was so cold. At first, I did not put two and two together, but then I realized I had become addicted to the pain medication. I went to my boss and explained what was happening. Luckily, she was very understanding, told me to call the doctor, and sent me home with the admonition to take the next day off.

I immediately went home and called the doctor. They could not believe I had stopped cold turkey with my medications. They told me it was dangerous to do that and that I needed to gradually wean myself off the medication. They called in another prescription and gave strict instructions on how many to take each day until I didn't need to take any more.

The hour between when I called and took the next pill was extremely hard for me. I felt like a junkie who could not wait for the next fix. Then it hit me like a semitruck. All the feelings that I had from years ago and the things that I did while doing drugs and drinking came crashing into my brain at two hundred miles an hour. I felt like a computer processing information too fast and was ready to blow up. I fell to my knees, sobbing while rocking back and forth, trying to gain back control.

The rush of guilt and shame for everything I had done hit me like a ton of bricks, and for the first time, I felt the weight of my past actions on my shoulders. You see, it wasn't just bad decisions anymore, as I had convinced myself over time. Now that I was a Christian, it was the weight of my sinful actions and what I had done, not just to myself, but to Jesus Christ.

It wasn't just living with the consequences that I had brought upon myself. It was realizing the full impact that it had on everyone around me. I was starting to fully understand my past actions.

My brain was going at warp speed, and my heart ached so bad that I thought I was going to have a heart attack. The emotional pain manifested itself into physical pain, and I couldn't stop crying. It was one of those ugly cries where you couldn't breathe, and you couldn't catch your breath. God was, once again, getting my attention and in a big way. I didn't really know what was going on, and it would take some time to make sense of it. Unfortunately, there is twenty-twenty vision in hindsight, right? My first thought was to call my mom. She somehow always knew what to say, and most of what she said made me feel better, but some of it was very convicting. Clearly, she was God's messenger. I don't think she fully understands, even to this day, that the words she said to me that day paved the way for the work the Lord wanted me to do and how impactful it was for me. They weren't just words of wisdom, but words that would completely change the course of my life. Again.

I called crying so hard I could barely talk. With patience, she finally got out of me what was wrong, and as she pieced together what had happened, she proceeded to tell me that Satan was angry that I was having a real relationship with Christ. He was trying to get at me in any way possible to throw me offtrack, and he seemed to be having some success. He was trying hard to take this moment to make me feel as worthless as possible. Satan's goal seemed to be to put doubts in my head and my heart about what Christ had done for me.

I thought things like, "After everything I had done, how could God love me? How could anyone love me? I had hurt so many people. It would be better to distance myself because apologizing wouldn't be good enough."

At that moment, I had a choice to make: to believe the lies going through my head or to cry out to God. God sent me His word and the strength I needed through my mother. She calmed me down by telling me that God is going to use this experience for His work, that He can't begin to use any of us until we are broken, and more importantly, that we understand that we are broken. I wasn't just broken at that moment, but completely shattered.

Over time, God opened my eyes to 2 Samuel 22. I read it over and over until it was ingrained into me as to who was my rock. I still read it to this day and give it out to other people who need encouragement.

David sang to the Lord the words of this song when the Lord delivered him from the hand of all his enemies and from the hand of Saul. He said this:

> The Lord is my rock, my fortress and my deliverer;
> my God is my rock, in whom I take refuge, my
> shield and the horn of my salvation. He is my

stronghold, my refuge and my savior- from violent people you save me. I called to the Lord, who is worthy of praise, and have been saved from my enemies. The waves of death swirled about me; the torrents of destruction overwhelmed me. The odds of the grave coiled around me; the snares of death confronted me.

In my distress I called to the Lord; I called out to my God. From his temple he heard my voice; my cry came to his ears. The earth trembled and quaked, the foundations of the heavens shook; they tremble because he was angry. Smoke rose from his nostrils; consuming fire came from his mouth, burning coals blazed out of it. He parted the heavens and came down; dark clouds were under his feet. He mounted the cherubim and flew; he sordid on the wings of the wind. He made darkness his canopy around him- the dark rain clouds of the sky. Out of the brightness of his presence bolts of lightning blazed forth. The Lord thundered from heaven; the voice of the Most High resounded. He shot his arrows and scattered the enemy; with great bolts of lightning, he routed them. The valleys of the sea were exposed and the foundations of the earth laid bare at the rebuke of the Lord, at the blast of breath from his nostrils.

He reached down from on high and took hold of me; he drew me out of deep waters. He rescued me from my powerful enemy, from my foes, who were too strong for me. They confronted me in the day of my disaster, but the Lord was my support. He brought me out into a spacious place; he rescued me because he delighted in me.

The Lord has dealt with me according to my righteousness; according to the cleanness of my hands he has rewarded me. For I have kept the ways of the Lord; I am not guilty of turning from my God. All his laws are before me; I have not turned away from his decrees. I have been blameless before him and have kept myself from sin. The Lord has rewarded me according to my righteousness, according to my cleanness in his sight.

To the faithful you show yourself faithful, to the blameless you show yourself blameless, to the pure you show yourself pure, but to the devious you show yourself shrewd. You save the humble, but your eyes are on the haughty to bring them low. You, Lord, are my lamp; the Lord turns my darkness into light. With your help I can advance against a troop; with my God I can scale a wall.

As for God, his way is perfect: The Lord's word is flawless; he shields all who take refuge in him. For who is God besides the Lord? And who is the Rock except our God? It is God who arms me with strength and keeps my way secure. He makes my feet like the feet of a deer; he causes me to stand on the heights. He trains my hands for battle; my arms can bend a bow of bronze. You make your saving help my shield; your help has made me great. You provide a broad path for my feet, so that my ankles do not give way.

I pursed my enemies and crushed them; I did not turn back till they were destroyed. I crushed them completely, and they could not rise; they fell beneath my feet. You armed me with strength for battle; you humbled my adversaries before me. You made my enemies turn their backs in flight, and I destroyed my foes. They cried for help, but there was no one to save them- to the Lord, but he did not answer. I beat them as fine as the dust of the earth; I pounded and trampled them like mud in the streets.

You have delivered me from the attacks of the people; you have preserved me as the head of nations. People I did not know now serve me, foreigners cower before me; as soon as they hear of me, they obey me. They all lose heart; they come trembling from their strongholds.

The Lord lives! Praise be to my Rock! Exalted be my God, the Rock, my Savior! He is the God who avenges me, who puts the nations under me, who sets me free from my enemies. You exalted me above my foes; from a violent man you rescued me. Therefore, I will praise you, Lord, among the nations; I will sing the praises of your name.

He gives his king great victories; he shows unfailing kindness to his anointed, to David and his descendants forever. (2 Samuel 22 NIV)

I called out to the Lord, and He saved me. He proved to me that day and over the next couple of days that no matter what happens, no matter what Satan does to try to bring us down, He is there holding our hand, and all we must do is squeeze it and ask for help. My mom said something in our conversation that, combined with the passage above, really helped put things back into perspective. She told me that God wanted to use me in a big way. She explained that my experiences can now be used to help people who have gone through what I have been through. She further explained that there was a recovery program for men at our church, but not for women. She told me to think about it and look into it. I would have never thought in a million years what God wanted for the next steps of my journey.

I thought and prayed about it and even journaled about it, asking for God's guidance for what He wanted me to do. What was the purpose of this major event in my life? It was amazing how quickly He answered me. I wrote two journal entries, and they were back-to-back. I asked one day and received the answer the next day.

May 6, 2012

A spiritual battle has been going on in me the last few days. My past addictions and discretions have been weighing heavily on me. Doubt has risen to the surface, and questions of my self-worth are forefront in my mind. As I am new in my faith, I am learning to rely heavily on God and to put my full trust in Him. I am worthy! Although I may not deserve God's love, I know that God loves me unconditionally.

Satan is attacking my new faith and trying to tear my faith apart. It will never work! I will rely and lean on my God and ask Him to strengthen me every minute, every second of every day. I may struggle, but with God at my side, I know that Satan will never win.

My struggle is not knowing which direction God wants me to go. Where do You want me, Lord, and

I will follow? Please show me the path You have planned for me. I know You have big plans for me, Lord, as Satan wouldn't be so eager to try and put distance between us. I thank You for being patient with me and softening my heart so I can now truly understand Your love. I believe You will never leave my side, and for that alone, I am eternally grateful.

May 7, 2012

God may have answered my prayers today. I got a call from the church, telling me they did not have a women's recovery group because they are looking for a leader. I may not be a mature-enough Christian to lead the group just yet, but I told them I would be very interested in helping get a group started. There is such a strong need for it, and since I need it, maybe God is showing me the path of where He wants me to be and serve Him. Since Satan has been attacking me with my own battles, I know God is going to use it for good. If I have to struggle in order to help other people and lead them to Christ, then I am willing to pay that price.

For the first time in my life, I feel like I have a purpose, and all I want to do is God's work, and I'm so excited. I just pray that God will continue to work through myself and my church to get this group started. God is so awesome and amazing! He does answer prayers.

Indeed, God answers prayers. I went from having no clue as to what God wanted me to do, to going through a complete breakdown, and then seeing some clarity in the direction God wanted to take me. God rescued me twice. And from those rescues came transformation to want to pay it forward and help others. I was rescued, and being rescued inspires rescuing.

Chapter 7
RECOVERY

When people hear the word *recovery*, the words *drugs* and *alcohol* will most likely come to mind. But recovery is not just about a substance-abuse problem; it is about recovering from a habitual sin problem. By using this term, we can start to see that recovery can be more than just substance abuse; it is about anything that enslaves us and separates us from God.

True recovery is freedom in Christ and getting rid of the strongholds that keep us enslaved to sin. True freedom involves more than just being sober in your habitual sin but involves a heart transformation from knowing Jesus Christ.

Over time, society has largely accepted the characterization of addictions as diseases. Therefore, many reading this book may be wondering and/or skeptical as to why *habitual sin* is being used to replace the word *addiction* in this book. Addiction may be a disease; however, that disease is our sin. It is not a disease in the sense that we catch or are born with alcoholism or drug addiction.

People tend to use the word *disease* as a crutch for avoiding taking responsibility for their choices. It is a choice to pick up that drink and then the next one and then the next one. It is a choice to snort that line of cocaine or to choose to have that third serving of food as a mask to cover up emotions. When we substitute the word *addiction* for *habitual sin*, it takes away the excuses and the lack of responsibility in using the word *disease* and puts the responsibility of our own choices and our sin back on us.

What is sin? Sin can be considered anything we do that goes against God's commandments. Edward T. Welch, in his book *Addictions: Banquet in the Grave*, stated that sin is ultimately against God. It is any failure to conform to the law of God in either action or attitude. It is not only the actions that get us into trouble, but also the mindset that we have going into those actions. For example, it is not a sin to drink alcohol; however, it is a sin to drink to excess. Anything in excess is considered a sin. One may say "I only had two glasses of wine." That is not in excess, but the mindset of those two glasses of wine was to drown the sorrows of that day, and instead of going to God for comfort and relief from those harsh emotions, this person went to alcohol. They went to get that immediate relief to take away their feelings. The mindset of why this person is drinking can be just as much a sin as drinking five glasses of wine just to have fun.

People often assume that sin is always a person's conscious choice to disobey God, that a person is always in complete control over saying yes or no to those choices. Often, addiction gives the appearance that the substance is in control. An example of that can be found in something as simple as watching a commercial. A person with an alcohol addiction only must see a vodka commercial on TV and find they are unable to resist getting up and getting that drink. It feels like the substance has taken control. I have been there too many times to count.

If you were anything like me, you would have made the decision not to drink or do drugs. You would have felt in control, putting your foot down, determined not to party that night. Then, within thirty minutes of making that decision, you would get invited to the bar. You might have dragged your feet a bit but, ultimately, decided to go. You convinced yourself it was okay to have a couple of drinks but have no drugs.

You found yourself at the bar, on your third drink, when one of your friends suggested having an after-party at their house. You were already feeling a little tipsy, and your willpower was slowly caving in. You decided to go, but you still resolved not to do drugs.

Upon entering the house, you saw drugs lined up on the coffee table. Before you knew it, your resolve crumbled, and it took no more than five minutes to do that first line. You knew the feeling: the moment you saw it, your mouth started to salivate, and your body craved the drugs. The cravings took over physically, and your mind lost control. Suddenly the smart decision you thought you had made just a few hours prior came crashing in at full speed. You finally realized the drugs were in control. But were they?

How did you get to that point? Let's see. Were you standing in your living room one day and suddenly started craving drugs so badly that you just had to start doing them? Or did you make choice after choice to pursue alcohol and drugs until your body became controlled by the substances?

Edward T. Welch further discusses this in his book:

> The disease model does not fit as well as we might think. The cravings and desires at the core of the addictive experience are not quite the same as an invading virus. If you catch a virus, you have no

choice. You don't want it, and you would be glad to be rid of it. Heavy drinking, however, doesn't just happen to us. Instead, the drinker feels there are payoffs—however temporary—to drunkenness. (There are for any sin.) In other words, addicts make choices to pursue their addiction.

As one experienced drinker observed, "When the desire to drink hits me, I feel like I am being pulled in different directions by two teams of horses."

"Which team wins?" asked a friend.

"Whichever one I say 'giddyap' to."

Even with all the associated misery, people drink because, on some level, drinking does something for them. Their drinking appears to be purposeful.

Coming to terms that addiction is habitual sin can be a new perspective for you. Maybe it is one that you are open to understanding, or maybe you are pushing it aside. There are differing viewpoints as to the definition of addiction and whether it is a genetic disorder or disease. If it is a disease, how do you catch it? No matter which approaches you take, the answer to freedom remains the same—Jesus Christ. It is your choice whether you want to follow Him and truly receive the pure freedom that He longs to give you. Using other terms such as *addict* or *addiction* tends to point toward the perspective that the problem lies within the body and not the heart. Habitual sin is a heart issue, and to repair the problem, you need a heart transformation that only Jesus Christ can provide.

God gave us free will to make the choice to follow Him. It wouldn't mean anything if He forcefully compelled us to love

Him. He wants us to freely choose him so that we can live a joyful and purposeful life.

The hardest part in starting your recovery and finding your freedom is realizing that you have a problem and admitting that the problem is not going to go away without some help. You cannot do it on your own. God used my neck surgery to get my attention and to show me that there was work to be done. He shows each of us through our unique understanding what it is that we need to lay at Jesus's feet to receive true freedom from sin enslavement. In the process of accepting that I had become dependent on the pain medication, a much-bigger door of realization was opened. The magnitude of what God was trying to show me was almost overwhelming. It tore across my soul like a hurricane hitting land and leaving a path of destruction so big I didn't even know how to begin healing.

Admitting that there was a much-bigger problem that I needed to address was hard. I needed to contact my church and ask about a recovery program for women. Admission to struggling with any type of addiction is scary. The feelings of shame and embarrassment invade the mind, and a battle of resistance begins to wage war internally. This ends up throwing the mind into a downward spiral.

God wanted me to take that step to becoming free and Satan wanted me to feel worthless so I would not take those steps. I eventually grabbed my head and fell to my knees in tears, not knowing what to do. I did not—no, I could not—let Satan win, as the only result would be to turn back to the one thing that is short-lived: temporary pleasure. God grants us these moments of clarity amid our darkest chaos. Sometimes, they are longer moments than others. These moments of clarity give us the ability to act upon our need to get help. So not only do we need to realize that we have a problem that we can't fix ourselves, but we also need to act upon that newfound knowledge.

If you are a believer and already attend a church, the first step would be to reach out to your church. It can be as simple as reaching out to a friend who can help pray for you and work with you to understand your needs and identify the right program. Some churches already have recovery programs in place, such as Celebrate Recovery or Setting Captives Free, which would be a good starting point for getting plugged in. There are several AA meetings across the nation that you can attend as well.

Bringing your sin and your struggles out of the darkness and into the light is a critical first step. Sin tends to hide in the darkness, where no one can see what you are doing. This also means that no one can help hold you accountable and be there to support you on your journey.

If you are not a believer in Jesus Christ, I pray that Jesus opens your heart to make that choice to follow Him. As stated earlier, He is the only answer to your freedom. Jesus is the only one who can bring you to live in the light instead of wallowing in a sea of darkness, where waves continuously crash down in an effort to drown you.

Find a Christ-centered recovery program to attend on a regular basis, one that teaches scripture and delves deep into understanding the meaning of a relationship with Christ. Alcoholics Anonymous or Narcotics Anonymous are in just about every city. I recommend you go to these meetings immediately if the need is urgent. They are plentiful, and more of those meetings are available at different time slots than you will find with a specific church-centered program.

Regardless, as soon as possible, find a church to attend near you, and get involved. Call the church office and share with them your struggles so that they can help you. They will facilitate getting connected and help to find and identify available meetings to attend, especially if they do not already have a supporting program.

There is one important caveat: please know that although Christ is the answer to finding your freedom from habitual sin, spiritual transformation and guidance cannot take place until you have safely gone through detoxification. There are several rehabilitation centers across the nation that can help you break the physical dependence on substances. The ideal place to go is a Christ-centered rehab center. Their ability and experience to help you through the detox stage in concert with spiritual support are very important. Your mind will not be able to focus on God if it is solely focused on the physical withdrawals.

After contacting my church about a women's recovery group, they pointed me in the direction of a program called Setting Captives Free. As I shared with my church my former and current experiences, they immediately asked me to start in the program and connected me with a mentor. Setting Captives Free is a Bible-based program that centers your focus on God and teaches you who you are in Christ. It teaches that when we choose anything other than Christ as our priority, it becomes a sin issue. It could be drinking excessively, drug abuse, overeating, money, careers, and many more things. I had a lot to learn.

Every time we choose to drink until we can't see straight, or we go straight to a whole pint of ice cream, we are choosing to go to things of this world instead of leaning on Christ. It taught me the meaning of living water and how Jesus is that living water and He is the only one who can quench our thirst.

There might have been many injustices that could have completely brought you to rock bottom. Maybe it was sexual and/or physical abuse when you were growing up or even in a relationship as an adult. Maybe it was losing someone so dear to your heart that the physical ache was overwhelming. These kinds of circumstances can crush you and completely break you. All you feel is pain and agony. The memories swarm in from every angle. It is hard not to want immediate relief from the pain and anguish even if it is only temporary. But we need to understand and believe that healing comes by fighting through the pain, leaning on Christ, and asking Him to give us the strength to get through the trials happening to us.

It's not fair that bad things happen to good people, but we live in an imperfect, fallen world, a world full of sin. All we can do is fall on our knees and ask God to relieve us of the pain and have hope that beyond this life, there will be a time where there will be no more pain and suffering. There will be no more tears. I know, easier said than done. This life is hard with its constant struggles. But if we can learn the truths and the tools to use to get through life the right way, then we can start to feel the peace, love, and joy of clutching to Christ's hand while He leads the way.

> So do not fear, for I am with you;
> Do not be dismayed, for I am your God.
> I will strengthen you and help you;
> I will uphold you with my righteous right hand.
> All who rage against you
> will surely be ashamed and disgraced;
> those who oppose you
> will be as nothing and perish.
> Though you search for your enemies,
> you will not find them.
> Those who wage war against you

will be as nothing at all.
For I am the Lord your God
who takes hold of your right hand
and says to you, Do not fear;
I will help you. (Isaiah 41:10–13)

Some of you are reading this and rolling your skeptical eyes. You may be thinking that I don't know you or understand your experience. Or perhaps you're hearing something similar in church and wondering the same thing. I used to think this way, and to be honest, there are a lot of people who will try to give you advice but really do not understand your experience.

They will sincerely, but self-righteously, tell you that Jesus can be your rock and that you will get through it. They will tell you that they will pray for you but, again, in a self-righteous way. Often, these types of Christians do not follow up with actions. Don't get me wrong; having people praying for you is one of the most important elements of recovery, but when presented in the wrong context, it is just not what you want or need to hear. You may want to tell them to just shut up. You sense more judgment from these Christians rather than understanding love. And it does not help that your mindset may be defensive because you are not ready to let go of that bottle or other dependency for comfort.

I have felt all these emotions, especially before I surrendered to Christ. My family would point me to Christ and get on me about going to church. They couldn't understand why I would make the choices that I did and why I couldn't just open my life to Christ and start being good. Keep in mind that these were the feelings that I was feeling and not necessarily my family's intentions. But nonetheless, it pushed me away because I felt they couldn't understand me.

I finally came to the place where I understood that not everyone was going to understand but that, if people were trying to point me to Christ and trying to give me advice on how to get through situations, it was because they loved me. Yes, some of the people I encountered were judgmental and self-righteous, and I had to learn that they are people too. And as much as I might not have agreed with them, it was their sin, to which they would need to answer, and not my own.

One day, my brother was preaching God's Word to a couple thousand high school students. I was lucky enough to see him teaching these kids. He told a story that I had heard before but from a perspective that really hit home. To this day, I still look at that moment of epiphany and wish I had realized it years earlier during my hard times. It was the story of the woman who was suffering from bleeding for twelve years and touched Jesus's robe for healing.

In this story, a man ran over to Jesus, asking Him to heal his sick daughter, who was twelve years of age. As Jesus walked, He had His disciples with Him, and a crowd of people had been following Him, wanting to see Him perform miracles and to hear Him preach. People were starting to crowd Him and the disciples as they continued to walk.

Picture this with me: you are at a concert, front and center of the stage, right down in the mosh pit. If you have ever been in that section of a concert, it is pure craziness. People are pushing you left and right; you start to sweat because you have a thousand people squished into a very small area designated for at most five hundred people. You have no idea who is next to you or in front of you, and you definitely don't know who is behind you. There are too many people pushing to get closer to the stage, trying to hear the music and get close to the band. This is what I picture when reading this story. It might not have been exactly like that, but there was a big crowd all trying to get close to Jesus.

So as Jesus was walking to this man's house to see his daughter, a woman came up behind Jesus and touched the bottom of His cloak. This woman had been bleeding for twelve years, and no one could heal her. Back in that day, when you had a health issue or a disease, you were labeled unclean and cast out from normal society.

As you can imagine, she snuck up in the middle of the crowd and crouched low, probably crawling on her knees to touch His cloak. She didn't want anyone to see her or know she was there, as she knew she would be mocked and chastised by the people. However, somehow, she had enough faith and belief in Jesus that she believed that if she could just touch His cloak, she would be healed — and she was. As soon as the woman touched the cloak, her bleeding stopped.

Jesus stopped immediately and asked, "Who touched my cloak?" Now the crowd was pressing in and crushing Jesus and the disciples. So many people were bumping and pushing; it was no surprise when Peter gently pointed out that everyone was pushing up against Jesus, and many most likely touched His cloak. Peter did not think twice about it, but Jesus knew what happened.

> But Jesus said, "Someone touched me; I know that power has gone out from me." Then the woman, seeing that she could not go unnoticed, came trembling and fell at his feet. In the presence of all the people, she told why she had touched him and how she had been instantly healed. Then he said to her, "Daughter, your faith has healed you. Go in peace." (Luke 8:46–48)

Keep in mind that this woman was an outcast from society. The last thing she wanted was to be in the spotlight. But her faith overcame her fear. She believed Jesus could heal her, and it was that faith that healed her. Although faith was one of the main points of the story, it is important to point out something else. Amid the overwhelming, crushing crowd, Jesus knew that the woman had touched His cloak.

No one else saw or understood the woman's years-long experience with her affliction. In fact, the people had more than likely cast her out to die with everyone else who was considered to be unclean. They did not understand her circumstances, but Jesus knew. He knew her experience and the state of her heart the moment she touched His cloak. He knew the level of her faith and that she was at rock bottom. She chose to believe in Jesus and to follow Him, knowing that He could, indeed, heal her.

Perhaps you are in the beginning stages of your recovery process, or maybe you have already gone through it, but remember that a lot of people will not understand your situation or experience; but Jesus knows. He knows everything you have gone through, done, and what has been done to you. He understands, and He still loves you. He wants to get to know you or get reacquainted with you.

Don't let the perception of "No one understands" impede your recovery process. Jesus will be right there waiting for you to lean on Him, and He will provide someone as His messenger who does understand and can relate to what you are going through.

Chapter 8
GUILTY SHAME

Do not be afraid; you will not be put to shame. Do not
fear disgrace; you will not be humiliated. You will forget
the shame of your youth and remember no more the
reproach of your widowhood.

—Isaiah 54:4 (NIV)

Satan's number one tactic for bringing us down is to highlight
and exploit feelings of guilt and shame. These feelings are
often recognized as a knot that is in your stomach and shoots
through your heart when you realize all the things you have
done. The knot originates as thoughts like ripples in the ocean
and builds until eventually they end up as fifteen-foot waves
crashing down on you.

Often, you are in denial about the building waves until they
thrash your body into a tumbling mess. You try to get to the
surface of the water so you can get a breath of fresh air, but
you soon don't know which way is up. Your lungs start to burn,
and panic starts to set in. You start to feel like you may not
live to see another day. Satan's goal is to keep you tumbling in
the water so you can't surface to catch your breath. He doesn't
want you to gain control and go back to knowing who you are
in Christ.

Shame can hinder you from finding that freedom in Christ and realizing that your value is in Him and not in the things of your past. For too long, I allowed shame to keep me from living out God's will for me. Feelings of worthlessness would creep into the small crevices of my mind and attach themselves to my core. Eventually, the personality I presented became a front for all my insecurities. I exaggerated my confidence to those around me so that no one would really know that I felt worthless inside; even further confusing my identity.

Rejection was one of my biggest fears. I experienced it in several ways: men who told me that I wasn't worth more than a "good night." Good "friends," themselves feeling rejection, turned on me after I left Florida by sending the message that I was no longer worth their time. It was manifested in the fear that in my new life, people would find out everything that I had done, or they would discover my flaws and cast doubt as to whether I could add value to a friendship. I pictured it in my head: the judgment of people finding out that I had done drugs and concluding that I was tainted goods.

There would be judging of my sexual promiscuity and thinking that I could no longer be "pure." But in my darkness, I was determined for that not to happen to me, and as a result, I pushed people away. I went from the one extreme of going from relationship to relationship to avoiding even the option to be in a relationship. The fear of rejection paralyzed and prevented me from being able to love and be loved.

It wasn't just about finding a husband; it was about completely shutting down the ability to love in the capacity that God calls us to love. I didn't love my friends or my family in accordance with God's commandments. We must set aside our fear of rejection and have faith in God. We may go through struggles in life, but we can't live life through a prism of fear, constantly seeking our hearts' desire through a distorted lens of reality. Fear of rejection will stop us in our tracks from ever reaching those desires. This is not what God wants from us or for us.

God wants us to step off that cliff in faith, knowing that He will catch us. The only way to overcome the shame and guilt we feel for our sins is to acknowledge that God is the only one who matters in our judgment. If we accept Jesus as our Lord and Savior, we are covered by His death on the cross. He is our redemption, our redeeming love. We are forgiven for our sins, past, present, and future.

My greatest challenge was continuing to ask for God's forgiveness every time I experienced feelings of despair and shame. And this is another tool of Satan: to cause us to doubt our forgiveness in Christ. To make us think that God could not possibly forgive us once and for all. But you see, continuing to ask for forgiveness from God multiple times causes Him pain and sorrow in the demonstration of our unbelief. We are, in our hearts and minds, invalidating His death on the cross by not accepting His promise of complete and final forgiveness. Our sins are washed clean as snow. There is no more blood to be spilled on those sins. The problem lies in whether we are willing to forgive ourselves.

> Peter replied, "Man, I don't know what you're talking about!" Just as he was speaking, the rooster crowed. The Lord turned and looked straight at Peter. Then Peter remembered the word the Lord had spoken to him: "Before the rooster crows today, you will disown me three times. And he went outside and wept bitterly. (Luke 22:60–62 NIV)

Forgiving ourselves is the key to unlocking the door to God's blessings and plans for us. It is a part of the healing process. If we are not able to forgive ourselves, then a darkness starts to brew in our hearts and leads the way to falling back into Satan's grasp. We can be our own worst enemy. The temptations start to get stronger and, left unchecked, will ultimately drown our emotions in something other than Christ. We need to be able to arrest our shameful thoughts and lay them at Jesus's feet. If God can love us enough to forgive our sins, then we need to be able to let go of our shame and move forward. God will use everything for good. Saint Peter is a classic example.

Peter loved Jesus with all his heart and promised to follow Jesus into eternity. Even after Jesus told him he would deny him three times, Peter refused to believe it. In his mind, there was no way he would deny the son of God, especially after everything he had witnessed. Yet later that night, as Jesus was arrested and brought in for trial, Peter did just that. In the chaos and commotion, Peter was asked by the crowd if Jesus was the man he had followed. Peter immediately denied it. Fear gripped him, and he was unable to boldly say he was a follower of Jesus. Peter's reaction to his fear revealed his own shameful state. Put yourself in Peter's sandals and imagine being a disciple of Jesus for three years. You have been in his presence day and night, learning from him, and realizing the love that you have for Him and knowing that He is truth. Peter gave up his career as a fisherman to follow Jesus and to become a fisher of men.

That takes a leap of faith and some serious trust. Yet Peter, when it came down to it, denied Jesus not once, not twice, but three times. I don't know about you, but the shame and guilt that would come pouring over me would be overwhelming. I think I would curl up in a ball in a dark room, never to show my face again. How could I face anyone, especially Jesus, when I had failed so miserably?

Yet Peter did not shut down or disappear. He continued, after Jesus's death, to disciple others and showed them the righteous path to follow. This tells us that he not only sought Jesus's forgiveness, but forgave himself, as well, which allowed him to live out God's will. We must not let our shame hinder us to the point of disobedience. Not only will we deny ourselves the blessings that God wants to give us, but we will also deny the people whom God wants us to help.

To give up shame means to look to Jesus. Our thoughts should be focused on Him and His redemption. God has redeemed us by His sacrificial actions and love. When we choose Jesus Christ, we are no longer slaves to our emotions and our thoughts. Knowing that God, even in our brokenness, sees the goodness in us creates an amazing sense of freedom. It took me a long time to come to this realization.

For the first few years, Satan held me captive in my thoughts of shame and guilt. It wouldn't take much to trigger flashbacks of my Florida days or even before then when I was in San Diego; something as small as a song on the radio would send me into a state of insecurity. These flashback memories of past shameful sins would start to play in my mind over and over, which would then trigger another set of memories. One of the memories that Satan always tried to use was my start of drug use after I returned from Florida. He tried to use this to bring me down and make me feel that I couldn't run from the drugs, that it was hard coded in my DNA and there was no way out and I might as well just give in to the temptations of pure bliss forever.

I came home from Florida thinking that I was pulling myself away from the drugs and the bad crowd. It was a good decision, but it was only the beginning. My habits and my way of thinking needed to change, as well. I no longer had the same access to drugs, and that helped as long as I did not have a connection. Well, that did not last long as I soon found a connection again. I was dating someone who had a friend who had access to cocaine. We were out partying one night, and there it was, spread out on the kitchen counter. It was a flashing big beacon of temptation.

The thoughts that went through my head were, unfortunately, pure excitement. I couldn't wait to do it again. I forgot the destructive path that I left behind in Florida, and the only thing my mind focused on was the feeling I was going to get after snorting that first line. The high that my body would feel was the only focus of my thoughts. The decision had already been made. I wasn't following Christ at this time, so I had no armor to put on me. I had no action plan for me to run away, and of course, my boyfriend at that time decided he was going to partake even though it wasn't a normal occurrence for him.

It seemed the deck was stacked, so why not, right? That was the start of another downward spiral, but this time, I knew better. The conviction and shame came a lot quicker this time but still didn't stop me until one event shook me enough that it stopped me in my tracks. We were partying one night, and I had made the commitment to meet my mom at an exercise boot camp early the next morning. But my desire to snort lines of coke was more important to me.

I remember telling myself multiple times that this was the last line because I had to get up early in the morning. But I couldn't say no every time another round was prepared. I eventually went to bed, but I only got a couple of hours of sleep before my alarm went off. My body was a wreck. I had a headache the size of Texas, and there was no way I was going to make the boot camp. Having to make that phone call to cancel on my mom was a wake-up call.

Disappointing my mom was the last thing I wanted to do. I couldn't tell her that I had stayed up all night doing drugs, but oddly enough, I felt I could tell her that I had too much to drink. That seemed to be a little bit more of an acceptable lie even though the point is I canceled on her regardless of the reason. But when we are addicted to certain behaviors, it is interesting how we rationalize one as being more acceptable than others.

My relationship with my parents was getting better, and the last thing I wanted to do was destroy it again. God's conviction quickly turned into condemnation. I felt sick to my stomach that whole day. Not only was my body going through a physical hangover, but my soul was going through a hangover of its own. The drugs were starting to undermine my efforts to repair my relationships. The shame and guilt that I felt lasted a long time and brought my insecurities back into play. This bout of drug use didn't last long, praise the Lord, but it still did damage to my soul.

Satan tried to bring me down again using my sense of shame to lower my self-worth and make me feel that I wasn't good enough for anyone. And I must admit that he succeeded for quite some time. But in the long run, we can claim Jesus Christ as our Lord and Savior and claim victory over our lives through Him. No longer will Satan be able to win the war. Are you ready to claim victory over your emotions of shame and guilt? Are you ready to climb up out of the muddy hole and into God's loving arms? No longer do we need to be slaves to our emotions. We must consistently lay them at Jesus's feet. We must forgive ourselves as Jesus forgave us so that we can walk forward into the light of victory.

> It is for freedom that Christ has set us free. Stand
> firm, then, and do not let yourselves be burdened
> again by a yoke of slavery. (Galatians 5:1 NIV)

Conviction comes from God, but condemnation comes from
Satan. God will convict our hearts when He feels we have
sinful behavior that is going to separate us from Him. It is that
feeling of wanting to lay out our sins and ask for forgiveness.
There are times, though, when Satan will capitalize on that
conviction and exploit our vulnerabilities to highlight our
shame and condemnation. It is a thin line between accepting
that we are no longer being convicted for our actions and
continuing to beat ourselves up by basking in the gloom and
guilt of our past actions. This is prime ground for Satan to
bring us down. Realizing where the line is drawn helps us to
overcome those thoughts before they do too much damage.

Jesus illustrates this line in the story of a woman who was
brought before him and accused of adultery. As she was
paraded in front of the crowd by a group of Pharisees, I could
only imagine the amount of shame and fear she must have felt.
As she was getting ready to be convicted of her crimes, Jesus
stepped in and began to write with his finger in the sand.

> At dawn he appeared again in the temple courts;
> where all the people gathered around him, and he
> sat down to teach them. The teachers of the law
> and the Pharisees brought in a woman caught in
> adultery. They made her stand before the group and
> said to Jesus, "Teacher, this woman was caught in
> the act of adultery. In the Law Moses commanded
> us to stone such women. Now what do you say?"
> They were using this question as a trap, in order to
> have a basis for accusing him.

But Jesus bent down and started to write on the ground with his finger. When they kept on questioning him, he straightened up and said to them, "Let any one of you who is without sin be the first to throw a stone at her. Again, he stooped down and wrote on the ground.

At this, those who heard began to go away one at a time, the older ones first, until only Jesus was left, with the woman still standing there. Jesus straightened up and asked her, "Woman, where are they? Has no one condemned you?

"No one, sir," she said.

"Then neither do I condemn you, Jesus declared. "Go now and leave your life of sin." (Luke 8 1–11 NIV)

Shame crouches around corners and lurks in the darkness to grab you at every opportunity.

Be alert and of sober mind, your enemy the devil prowls around like a roaring lion looking for someone to devour. Resist him, standing firm in the faith, because you know that the family of believers throughout the world is undergoing the same kind of sufferings. (1 Peter 5:8–9)

In the darkness of our sin, shame is internal, yet the moment we get exposed, shame magnifies itself ten times over. Your face starts to flush, and the temperature increases instantly. Your heart feels like it is going to pound out of your chest, and you want to crawl into a hole where you can't ever be seen. I could only imagine this is what this woman felt as she was pulled in front of a crowd of strangers and humiliated as someone who broke the law and was not worthy.

I have no idea what Jesus wrote in the sand since it wasn't stated, but the story was very powerful in turning the tables on the Pharisees and showing the sin within their own lives. Jesus does not condemn, and He tells us not to judge one another. It is not our burden to carry. We should not be condemning others for their sins when we have our own sin to worry about.

If you are like me, a lot of my guilt, shame, and embarrassment came from my self-condemning thoughts, but Jesus is the only one who can judge us on the day of judgment. We place this extra burden of people's thoughts and opinions on our shoulders when there is no need for it. Jesus doesn't shame us, nor does He use guilt to force us into doing things. Jesus is about providing love and forgiveness and the ultimate gift of grace. Jesus is the only one whom we should be focusing on for our approval and our value. When feelings of shame send us into that downward spiral, we need to call out to the Lord, put Him as our focus, and use it as a shield to help protect against those negative emotions that separate us from the blessing of a relationship with Christ.

Just like the woman caught in adultery, Jesus forgave our sins and told us to go and sin no more. We need to have faith that God will use our sinful past for good. I have finally gotten to the point where I thank God every day for allowing me to go through everything I have because, had I not, I wouldn't be able to help other women tear through that veil of darkness and see the light of hope.

You may be in the beginning stages of healing, or you have long since found your freedom, but wherever you are in your struggles, God has a purpose and a divine plan for you. Our experiences allow us to see the brokenness in other people more clearly and understand the struggles that they are going through. Jesus has allowed us to go through our own circumstances so that we may be that messenger for someone else. We understand the pain. We understand the surrender that is needed. We understand the struggles. We understand the shame, and we can or will understand that light of freedom that comes after that exhausting climb out of the pit.

We need to continue to keep our eyes open and attuned to thoughts full of shame and condemnation. And we need to arrest those thoughts and lay them at Jesus's feet every single time. That is how we become free from the guilt and shame that Satan tries to conjure up in our hearts. Knowing who we are in Christ diminishes the lack of security in who we believe we are.

> Therefore, there is now no condemnation for those who are in Christ Jesus. (Romans 8:1 NIV)

Chapter 9
TRUE LOVE

Love—love was the one thing that I was so desperately seeking. My mind reeled with the thought of how I could have gotten it so wrong. I had been looking for a man to fill that void in my heart, thinking that if I could just find someone who would love me unconditionally, then I would be perfectly happy—that person who would accept me just as I am.

My priority was to find someone with whom I could come home and talk about my day. When there was a bad day, he would wrap his arms around me, comfort me, and tell me everything was going to be alright. I needed that security of knowing that I was valued. It gave me purpose. I wanted to mean something in this world. If I had a husband and a family, then I felt that would give me the value so desperately needed. There is a misconception that happiness is to be sought and found within the walls of this world and among men. A man was on my pedestal, and a man was my god.

It wasn't until I was rescued and started to build that relationship with Jesus that I finally realized that I had a false sense of the meaning of love. I had been searching for something to fill that void, and I had tried everything within this world to overcome the loneliness I felt, only to learn that the answer was not of this world. It was found in Jesus Christ. God is love.

He embodies it and gives it unconditionally to His children. True love was found within God and is God. Love is God's very essence.

Romans 12:9–21 (NIV) states this:

> Love must be sincere. Hate what is evil; cling to what is good. Be devoted to one another in love. Honor one another above yourselves. Never be lacking in zeal, but keep your spiritual fervor, serving the Lord. Be joyful in hope, patient in affliction, and faithful in prayer. Share with the Lord's people who are in need. Practice hospitality. Bless those who persecute you; bless and do not curse. Rejoice with those who rejoice; mourn with those who mourn. Live in harmony with one another. Do not be proud, but be willing to associate with people of low position. Do not be conceited. Do not repay anyone evil for evil. Be careful to do what is right in the eyes of everyone. If it is possible, as far as it depends on you, live at peace with everyone. Do not take revenge, my dear friends, but leave room for God's wrath, for it is written: "It is mine to avenge; I will repay," says the Lord. On the contrary: "If your enemy is hungry, feed him; if he is thirsty, give him something to drink. In doing this, you will heap burning coals on his head." Do not be overcome by evil, but overcome evil with good.

By this definition, it was clear that I had no clue about love and what it meant. It was all about me and what someone could provide for me. When I met someone, I would ask myself, "Does this person give me that butterfly feeling and make my heart go pitter-patter?" If they didn't, there would be no interest. It was a constant feeling of joy and happiness for which I was searching. I think we all know that a constant state of happiness is far from possible, yet we continue to chase it like a lost red scarf blowing in the wind.

As I was thinking about this, I heard a message at church on sincere love. And wow, God really spoke to me through that sermon. The pastor talked about the four myths of love and what the biblical answers are to those myths.

Myth 1

Love is just *a feeling*

The tendency of this world is to believe that love comes naturally. When people get divorced or separated, I hear a lot of people say, "People fall in and out of love all the time." But love is a choice that we have to make every day. We need to ask ourselves, are we choosing to love those around us?

Love is hard and can be difficult, but it is about making a choice to love through those hard times and to work at our relationships. Imagine if God got upset with us, like we do with others, for the way we live our lives or the decisions that we make? Like us, He may very well lose His feeling of love for us, and then what? Can you imagine God deciding not to love us because He "fell out of love" over our choice to sin? No, of course not. That would completely invalidate the whole purpose of the Gospel.

God chooses to love us unconditionally. He chooses to bless us when we are obedient and to shower his peace and comfort into our souls through the Holy Spirit. When we are feeling down, He is there to lift us up. When we are completely broken, He is there to say I will show you the way. He does all those things because He chooses to love us.

For us, love is like a roller coaster; it is sometimes a hard, slow climb up the hill. You can almost hear the *click, click, click* of the chain pulling you to the top. But when you get to the top and come over the crest, the drop is absolutely thrilling. Our hands, suddenly, come up in the air, and as the wind whips into our faces, we are smiling and giggling uncontrollably. There is nothing like it. Then we know that all the hard work of loving is well worth the effort.

Constantly chasing this feeling of butterfly love was the goal in my life. Has it been like this in your life? Do you feel that way now? Have you chased the impossible feeling of constant happiness, only to be sorely disappointed? Each time we are disappointed, it feels like plunging down a steep cliff and feeling every scrape and bruise, maybe even some broken bones. We get to the bottom and look up with teary eyes at what seems to be an impossible climb back to the top. We become gun-shy at taking another chance only to be hurt again. Our confidence and self-esteem take another hit. Some of us might give up for a while; and some of us, stubborn and hardheaded, start that climb again, only to fall over and over.

How do we get past the point of disappointment, of giving up and trying to move on to the next thing? We understand that God is love and it is His purpose for us to choose to love each other. We may even have the head knowledge of how tough it is to love like that. The knowledge that it is a choice escapes a lot of us when the world we live in bombards us with messages that encourage self-centeredness to do whatever makes us happy.

There will be times of disappointment, but our success in working through it will increase significantly if we realize it is a choice within our control. Love is not *just* a feeling; it is a sacrificial choice, and the result of that choice is pure joy, but only with God. Directing our love to God instead of man is our only hope to satisfy the needs of our human souls.

Myth 2

Love just happens. We cannot help it; we have no control over it. We cannot help who we fall in love with

For a long time, I had this same misconception: that I would just know it when I saw it, right? My thought process through the years has always been that love just happens. People talk about love at first sight, but is that true? If we are not consistently choosing to love through the roller coaster of our feelings, then how can we be in love? Maybe, just maybe, we have fallen in and out of lust instead of love. I know that I have. This definition of love just blew my mind and changed my whole perspective on the true meaning of love. We need to understand the biblical meaning of true love to fully benefit from the blessings of God's love.

There is a story in the Bible of Amnon and Tamar. They were half-brother and half-sister, and Amnon was King David's son. Over time, Amnon fell in love with Tamar to the point he became obsessed and felt that he had to have her, so he devised a plan of trickery. He pretended to be sick and asked Tamar to go in and comfort him. He forcefully had his way with her even after she pleaded with him to think about what he was doing. Afterward, he was full of rage and hatred over what had transpired with Tamar. You see, Amnon was not really in love with Tamar; he was in lust. He did not understand the concept of true love. Amnon had a sense of entitlement that he should be able to fulfill his desires no matter the cost to anyone else. He demanded that he not go a second without fulfilling his needs and desires because of his position within the kingdom.

How often do we have the overwhelming compulsion to do whatever it takes to get what our heart desires? Have you ever felt something for someone and then either thrown yourself way out there to get their attention or devised a plan to gradually gain their attention by adjusting your personality to fit theirs? If you are successful, then before he or she knows it, you have conquered your quest of fulfilling your own desires. We may not devise a plan such as Amnon's, but there is a parallel in his story. It is base human nature to be selfish and self-centered, to have and cater to that feeling that we deserve happiness in this world and that we are entitled to it at all costs.

I cannot begin to tell you how many times I did things just to fit in with the group of the guy that I wanted to be with. Adjusting who we are is not the answer to fulfilling our happiness, because when you really look at it, love does not just happen. There is a part of us that will make unnecessary adjustments because we think the person in this group will make us happy, and when they don't, we jump into another group. We adjust our personalities to match what we think they want and then onto the next group, until one day, we wake up and realize we have no idea who we are. What do we really want in our lives? What really makes us happy and brings us joy beyond the men that we put up on pedestals? By the time I left Florida, my name was just a name. I no longer had an identity that was associated with my birth name of Courtney. Love was not happening for me, and I couldn't figure out why.

Ultimately, I realized the answer—God's love is consistent and unconditional. I still can't fathom that thought. It makes me speechless to think that even after all the things that I have done or said or still decide to do—the things that separate me from God—God continues to choose to love me. I don't think I will ever be able to fully comprehend that knowledge until I am in heaven. Just think about that for a moment. If

God chooses to love me unconditionally after all the drugs that I have done, after the sexual promiscuity, after repeatedly seeing my deceitful heart, after my acute self-centeredness, which allowed me to walk over anyone to get what I wanted, then I have no other choice but to believe that I have found love and that I am loved. And the good news is that His love extends to and is available to everyone, including you, dear reader. You are loved. You may not understand this concept or maybe you do, but you are loved unconditionally. Tears roll down my smiling face just thinking about the grace that God has given me, the grace that is built from His foundation of love. If God can continue to love me even after my past and for whatever I might do in the future, He can love you, too, no matter what your circumstances. You just have to open your heart and believe.

Myth 3

Love is about getting what we want. It is all about feelings

We are selfish in nature, so instinctively, I think that we think of love as pleasing ourselves. Isn't it about how it makes us feel? When you ask someone why they love someone, isn't the typical response something like "Well, they make me feel good, they love me, they value me, they are beautiful." It's all about how they make us feel, but love should be done more outwardly, and it needs to be in more of a sacrificial manner.

> But I tell you, love your enemies and pray for those who persecute you. (Matthew 5:44)

> For God so loved the world that He gave His only begotten Son. (John 3:16)

Throughout the Bible, God tells us that love is supposed to be sacrificial. It is critical to investigate our own lives and determine whether we are putting conditions on our love or whether we are being purely sacrificial with our love.

This myth ties in with all the other myths when it comes to thinking that love is all about us and our self-centered needs, in how we focus on how it makes us feel on getting what we want and what others can provide for us. When I told you the story about my friend and the loss of her brother, I demonstrated that we could live our lives in a way that prioritizes our needs and not the needs of others. This is the opposite of what God teaches in His word. God's number one commandment is to love Him and our neighbor. Love is what He wants us to pour out into this world. Love is making sure the other person gets a glimpse of God's glory, not of what we want or desire. It is not about us. Imagine a world where others thought more of others and living God's way of truth and love than living to please themselves. What a world that would be!

Myth 4

If we love, then love is accepting of everything

This is a big question: Are we called to be tolerant in everything anyone does because we need to sacrificially love? The answer is no. Many people equate tolerance and unconditional love with acceptance and approval. But it is important to remember that God's love is based on truth and nothing else.

It is possible to unconditionally love someone while not agreeing with their choices in how they live. We should not respond in a negative, judgmental way. Instead, we have a responsibility to gently "call out" our brothers and sisters in Christ to let them know that because we love them, we need to tell them what they are doing is wrong. This is often difficult, but if God's love is based on His truth, then we must be obedient as it demonstrates our understanding of the difference between sincere, unconditional love and the perceived acceptance of sinful behaviors.

We cannot refrain from admonishment simply because they may not like us anymore. Again, because it is not about us, it is about them. And likewise, if we are on the receiving side of admonishment, we need to avoid being defensive and investigate the sincerity of their words, as well as our own hearts for any truth to the matter.

One of the side results of being rescued by God is a new desire to help others. It took me a long time to figure out that everything that I was trying to bring to my life is found in God. When I did find it, I wanted nothing more than to spread the good news. I eventually ended up helping lead a women's recovery group for my church. It is a hard, dark ministry, especially when so many of the women are deep in darkness and only get occasional slivers of light from God. Even then it seems impossible for them to grasp.

There was one lady who had started coming to our group. She has struggled with a crack addiction and drinking for over fifteen years with occasional spurts of sobriety, only to fall deep once again into the abyss of darkness that has a stronghold on her life. Even worse, she thought she deserved it. Her self-esteem was nonexistent.

My heart broke for her because I had once been there, not to the same depth of darkness, but most certainly, I identified with the feelings of worthlessness and being undeserving of God's grace and love. She also struggles with homosexuality and hates herself for being attracted to women, but at the same time, she doesn't understand why she can't get rid of the compulsion to pursue this attraction. She intellectually understands that she is a child of God, yet she struggles with fully surrendering to Him.

She has moments of sobriety and resolve where she is on fire for God, and her real identity comes through. But the demons are too strong for her to fight on her own, and without full surrender, she eventually falls and stumbles back into darkness.

I love this woman dearly, and she has a special place in my heart. But loving her means that I can't accept her lifestyle of sin and that I have a responsibility as a child of God and as her mentor to lovingly tell her in truth that her lifestyle is full of sin. Continually turning her to Christ is my responsibility, but the rest is up to her and God. What a fine line that is for someone who wants to love unconditionally but knows that love means to love the person but draw the boundaries in overlooking the sin.

Sometimes, the only thing love requires is prayer and pointing back to God's truth when people reach out. Setting boundaries is hard but comes with the answer to the myth. Love does not require condoning different people's opinions and being tolerant if it goes against God's Word. We can love that person by giving them tough love and loving them where they are.

The one thing I am learning in leading a recovery group is realizing what I put my parents through all those years. They knew what it meant to love according to God's Word. They prayed for me but stuck to their decision in making me pull myself out of the hole that I put myself in. Tough love requires God's strength and being able to take a step back and say "There is nothing I can do for you as that would enable you to continue in your behaviors. But instead, pray and let you know I am here for you when you decide to walk in the light once again. Until that time, you are on your own."

Love requires faith and truth. Without faith and believing that God is love, there is no real understanding of what true love can provide. God can provide that stability of peace and joy that we so long for, but that only comes with believing that God is love. He embodies love. He embraces love, and He promises love. Once I opened my eyes to this fact and understood, my world was turned upside down, and I had my true aha moment.

After everything I have done, I know that God's love is the answer for my future, and it is the answer for your future, as well. We just need to get away from the notion of what love is in today's world and substitute it for the biblical definition, which states that love equals a choice to commit to consistent sacrificial actions based on the truth of God's Word. Once we can do that, then we are on the way to full recovery in our freedom through Jesus Christ.

Chapter 10
WHO AM I?

When I embrace the truth that the foundation of my
identity is the fact that I have been created in the image
of God, it gives my life great dignity, value, security,
significance, and purpose.
—Pastor Kent Sparks, Beachcities Community Church

Thoughts were dancing around in my mind when I woke
up in the morning, knowing I had scheduled four hours to
write that day. I planned to write about who we are in Christ
and the identity that we should build in Jesus. I was outlining
what I wanted to say as I straightened my hair for church that
morning. I walked into church and looked down at the sermon
outline and saw that it was titled "Do you know who you are?"

My eyes moistened as I knew God had been laying this
issue on my heart to share; now here was confirmation of
the importance of this topic. It is one of the most important
concepts to understand to have a fulfilling relationship with
Christ. We cannot become free from our enslavement to sin if
we do not know our true identity.

If I were to ask you "Who are you?" What would be your
response? It seems a simple question, but it becomes more
difficult when you know the meaning and the power behind

the question. Most of you would start to answer something like "Well, I'm a mother of two" or "I am an accountant." You might tell me where you live and maybe even tell me about your hobbies, but is that really you? Is your identity wrapped up in your career or your family? Do you rely solely on who you are in the world based on your functional purpose?

If you were to lose your job or career, would you lose yourself amid not knowing what you were going to do next? If you were to lose your family or your friends, would you experience an identity crisis? If you strip away the possibility of answering the question with a functional purpose, then how would you answer?

The answer should be based on what we want to emulate in this world. For me, my identity is in Christ. I am far from perfect but who strives to live a life that glorifies Christ's name. As a believer in Christ, your identity should be in your heavenly Father since you were created in His image. Your value becomes intrinsic as opposed to functional when you truly lay your life down to follow Christ. Too often, society is used as a barometer to gauge what is viewed as significant and to get confirmation of identity: for example, a well-paying job or career as defined by others. Are you married? Do you have kids? The perception of our culture today relies on materialistic aspects of our world and the confirmation of others saying well done. I, like so many others, succumbed to this pressure and found myself trapped in this satanic web of identity deception.

For far too long, I found my identity to be amid whether or not I had a man, family, and friends. More importantly, I thought my value was in what other people thought of me. I felt that I had no value if it was just me. My identity was wrapped up in my social status. I believed that a large group of friends was a measure of popularity and, therefore, meant that I was wanted and accepted, and it spoke directly to my self-worth.

Most of these feelings and emotions stemmed from my childhood and not understanding the true meaning of love. This partly derived from experiences where I was called names and ostracized from the groups from which I craved acceptance. All it did was increase my heart's desire for it, magnifying the acceptance within a social circle that I was going to aim for in life. That was my ultimate goal. I dreamed of having an unlimited number of friends. I remember even telling someone that I had enough friends to choose a new friend each day to hang out with and not run out for a year. I was full of pride as I had finally conquered my goal. The perception I had of myself was that I was the girl whom everyone wanted to party with. No longer would I be the outcast. No longer would I be picked on and shamed. Wow, what a broken mess my heart was in.

Self-perception determines your identity and your self-direction. My pastor once said some profound words that sunk deep down into my soul. How we view ourselves can be good and can also be very damaging, but most importantly, it determines how we are going to live our lives. My self-perception was full of insecurities, so I was driven to act in ways that would bring a level of acceptance that would replace my bucket of self-doubts with a bucket of inspiring admiration. My goal was to be a chameleon and blend in with whatever group I thought would pay attention to me. The problem with that is that I would change my appearance and behavior to whatever they perceived to be cool and accepted.

In today's culture, it is not unusual for a woman's identity to be wrapped up in their sexuality. The media plays a large part in that, between pushing women to be a model size 0, to promoting the wearing of skimpy bikinis at the beach. The image is portrayed that a woman's value is increased when you have that nice body, you dress sexy, and you look young and flawless. It is no longer accepted to be just who you are. The saying "As long as you are beautiful on the inside, then nothing else matters" doesn't seem to be demonstrated. It is worse today than ever before, and I fell into that trap. My level of acceptance needed to be fed, and that meant I followed the crowd in wearing the sexy clothing with the short shorts and the low-cut shirts. Carl's Jr. commercials used to portray this concept to a T by using scantily clad models eating hamburgers and using their sex appeal to lure in the business. Sex sells, right? Over time, this behavior desensitizes people and begins to blur the lines of decency and right from wrong. Too many of us fall into this pit of putting our identity in what others think and what is accepted. If the consensus agrees that sex sells, then why not start to project a woman's value to be sexual? Our identity starts to become a matter of public and/or business definition.

Our minds can get confused with the whirlwind of perceptions that we have of ourselves, especially depending on the settings in which we find ourselves. My insecurities would dictate how I acted in public, which—and let's be honest—was not superb. The choices that we make will either dictate consequences or result in blessings. The choices that I made were feeble and resulted in my sense of self-value degrading every day.

Thoughts of being a better person would take over and bring me into a deep depression. I so desperately wanted to be the person my parents would be proud of and, better yet, someone of whom I could be proud. Yet I didn't know how to change. I thought of myself as a weak individual who tried too hard to gain people's love. Doubt would creep into my soul as to whether anyone really loved me or could love me the way that I desired. My self-perception dictated the choices that caused me to negatively overcompensate for my shortcomings. My perception was that I had no value and would end up alone.

Loneliness is a powerful fear that drives us to put so much of our identity into what others think of us. We are wired to have that relational component to love and be loved. We were made in God's image. Think about that for a moment. To be made in God's image means God created us to be just like Him.

If God wired us to crave relationships, then that means that God craves relationships. He craves relationships with us. If we can redirect our focus on fulfilling our loneliness with a relationship with God, then it shouldn't matter what others think of us. We can finally realize that we are not alone, nor were we ever alone. It took me a long time to figure that one out.

It turned out that God was with me the whole time and my value was in Him. But realizing something and growing into really understanding it and internalizing it takes time. In that beginning process, my identity switched from needing a man and a family to my career being my identity. So even when I fully surrendered my heart to the Lord, I was building my value and identity in something other than the Lord. I had given up the need for a man; indeed, I felt it was a sacrifice for God, but this led me to mistakenly think that God was leading and blessing me in my career as a reward for that sacrifice.

Proud moments would envelop my identity and take over my entire being. I loved climbing up that corporate ladder no matter what the cost was to me. My identity relied upon the title and status that I thought I had the privilege of conquering with God's blessing.

Moving up in my career was always part of the plan. Work hard to get where you want to be. Make yourself proud and make your family and friends proud. Just keep working. Those were my thoughts when I was offered a position as a senior financial analyst with a bank. Going from a small private company to a large public company was the next step for me. Soon after I started, I was promoted to an impressive assistant vice president of the mortgage division. In my mind, I was important, and I was going places; however, the working conditions slowly began to wear on me.

Working eighty hours a week on top of trying to serve at church was just overwhelming. Working until midnight several days a week with no light at the end of the tunnel was draining. My heart was starting to change on whether it was worth climbing the corporate ladder just to make my identity even more impressive. My purpose in life was to work hard and create that high status within this world.

My purpose should have been living a life dedicated to Christ so that I might bring other people to know the love and truth of God. I was still missing the spiritual boat. I was still seeking that love and approval that I craved. I had just redirected it into another pursuit.

Stressful situations tend to bring attention to different perspectives that we never really thought about before. My goals for so long were to reach the top of the food chain within the accounting industry. I never thought of anything else. God started to put on my heart the desire to change gears. A change from the stressful climbing of the corporate ladder to a regular job working eight hours a day so that I could focus more on helping others in ministry.

This would mean possibly taking a pay cut and demotion in title. *Eek!* I soon realized that money also fueled my identity. I never thought it did until it made me sick to my stomach to think of giving up the money, the money that I worked so hard to earn and my annual bonus. What a reality check. My thought process was to rationalize reasons to "hang in there" with my current job until bonuses were paid out in a few months, and then I would find a new job.

But God wanted to strip away my thoughts of money too. He wanted to make sure that my newly realized identity and dependencies were going to be completely in Him and not my career or money. God was calling me to do one thing, but my love for money was preventing me from obeying His will for me. My identity was now wrapped in the functional rewards of my career. What was I supposed to do? Who was I without my big shot job? But eventually, God laid it on my heart to take my career off the pedestal on which I had placed it.

It was the hardest thing I ever decided to do, but I eventually ended up quitting my job and giving up my potential bonus and all without a new job in sight. This was completely new for me. God wanted to clearly change and mold my perspective of who I thought I was and realign it with Him, but it had to be my choice.

God was trying to get it through my thick head that my worth was unrelated to my function or performance. It was linked to Him. God wants us to choose to have a relationship with Him. He wants us to choose to believe in Him enough to obey Him. After long bouts of prayer and a lot of anxiety, I decided to obey God in everything He wanted for me. I was jumping into the unknown, and I was terrified. It is one thing to say you have faith and another thing to act upon that faith. I was going to walk by faith and not by sight.

I made the jump and decided to quit my job. I was terrified to go down that path. I was truly going on faith as I didn't have any idea when I would have a job or if I would be able to pay my bills when the money ran out. I had enough savings built up to last me about three months, but I knew if God wanted me to be obedient, He would provide for me.

I ended up taking six weeks off to decompress and to refocus my life on Christ. As it turned out, God blessed me with the time that I needed and ultimately provided a job that exceeded my expectations. It was the best six weeks of my life. Upon realizing that I had just become free, I truly felt like an eagle soaring through the sky, with its wings spread out, and feeling the wind in its face. Free from carrying the burden of putting status and money up on a pedestal.

My identity became my value in Christ and not something I did or earned. It turned from a functional identity into an intrinsic identity. My accomplishments or sense of acceptance finally had nothing to do with who I thought I was or could be. I finally understood that I was a child of God, and my performance in this world is not going to change my value in Christ.

My understanding was finally grounded in my heart and not in my head. God provided me with a job that gave me the work/life balance that I so desperately craved and still provided a management position that I am proud and passionate about. What a truly amazing God we have.

The real message here is about letting go of past failures, past hurts, and old ways of thinking. The acknowledgment and admission to ourselves that we have failed in the past with controlling our actions help us to move to that next cornerstone in our life. It opens our eyes to how to make the right decisions. And for us to take those steps in the right direction, we have to change our self-perception.

Dwelling on feelings of not being worthy and viewing ourselves as failures will be reflected in our actions. How we perceive ourselves intertwines with the direction of our lives. And we often get stuck in this pattern because our hearts and our minds are out of sync.

Intellectually, we have the knowledge that our value is in Christ, but what does that mean? How does Christ view His followers? The key is in connecting the intellectual head knowledge with a heart transformation. It is the key to building up our belief and faith in Christ. Changing one's self-perception from negative to positive can be challenging and difficult, but it can be done. God speaks about this very topic several times in the Bible.

He tells us that we are a masterpiece. He created us in a unique way so that we can stand out in our beautiful way from everyone else. We can fulfill His specific purpose uniquely designed for us as individuals. God does not make mistakes when creating us. We are who we are because God has a special plan for each of us. You were not born by mistake or an accident, because you are a child of His.

> For we are God's handiwork, created in Christ Jesus
> to do good works, which God prepared in advance
> for us to do. (Ephesians 2:10 NIV)

We have a heavenly Father who loves and adores us. His love is unconditional, and we are His children. We may have earthly parents, but God is our ultimate sovereign Father, and in the end, we will need to answer to Christ. Just as we want to please our parents and make them proud, we should also strive to seek and make God proud. We are special to Him. Among the billions of people in this world, God knows our name. He knows how many hairs we have on our head. He knows every one of our hurts and understands our struggles. He knows all our victories and loves us each individually as if we were His only child.

> See what great love the Father has lavished on us, that we should be called children of God! And that is what we are! The reason the world does not know us is that it did not know him. (1 John 3:1 NIV)

When our value and identity is in Christ, we become conquerors. This was especially true for me and the life path that I chose for myself. I had to claw my way out of that muddy pit and conquer the demons that wanted to knock me down and keep me down. You might feel the same way.

We go through so many struggles and see so much suffering in the world. It is easy to feel completely defeated and surrender to the desire to give up. It feels like you are climbing a steep mountain as you slowly stumble to the ground in exhaustion. It is critical in those times to remember that in Christ we are conquerors. In Christ, we have strength. With Christ in our lives, we can do anything because He will provide the strength that we need. No problem is too big or small for God. And with Him on our side, we can overcome any obstacle that comes into our paths. We are conquering warriors in God's army.

> No, in all these things we are more than conquerors through him who loved us. (Romans 8:37 NIV)

As a child of God, we are free from condemnation. The destructive thoughts that go through our minds make us feel unworthy and undeserving to be a child of His, and these need to be given to God. Through Christ, we are a new being, a new creature. No longer do we need to condemn ourselves because Jesus Christ will never condemn us. We can lay our guilt and shame at Jesus's feet because we have been forgiven.

The blessing of knowing Christ becomes the freedom that we can feel from the heavy load of condemnation that we once carried on our shoulders. It is a process to change our perspective, but knowing how God views His children and understanding that our identity is in Christ give us the freedom to be able to put into action positive thoughts, ultimately overcoming negative thoughts.

> Therefore, there is now no condemnation for those who are in Christ Jesus. (Romans 8:1)

We are chosen by the grace of God to be a part of His kingdom. God wants everyone to join His kingdom no matter what our past may be. If your past is anything like mine, His grace forgives us and changes our heart's desire to be for Him instead of the darkness of this world. Grace is the unconditional forgiveness that is given to us even when we don't deserve it.

God tells us our past does not matter; it is what we do now and in our future that matters. If we accept Christ into our lives as Lord and Savior, we are sealed by His power and given grace to be able to be connected with God. We are chosen to be His child. God is our acceptance and love. As I have thought about my past desires of wanting to be loved and accepted, the realization has come to me that God has always accepted me. It was I who was not accepting Him. I was doing the one thing to God that I feared people would do to me: rejection. This was one of those aha moments that come to me and are the switches that shine the light on our darkness.

> Praise be to the God and Father of our Lord Jesus Christ, who has blessed us in the heavenly realms with every spiritual blessing in Christ. For he chose us in him before the creation of the world to be holy and blameless in his sight. In love he predestined

us for adoption to sonship through Jesus Christ, in accordance with his pleasure and will- to the praise of his glorious grace, which he has freely given to us in the One he loves. In him we have redemption through his blood, the forgiveness of sins, in accordance with the riches of God's grace that he lavished on us. (Ephesians 1:3–8)

We can be strengthened by the power of God. In our weakness, we are strong. With God by our side, we can get through anything. As I was going through my struggles of changing from my old self to my new self in Christ, I needed God every step of the way. He holds our hand throughout the day as a reminder that He is with us. We just have to remember to lean on Him.

God's character is just amazing to me as I go through these verses reminding me of the blessings of following Him. He cares about us. Knowing that we are unconditionally loved, and we can do anything through Christ strengthens us and provides comfort and contentment in the midst of this crazy world. We are powerful, and we are strong with Christ by our side.

For who is God besides the Lord? And who is the Rock except our God? It is God who arms me with strength and keeps my way secure. (Psalm 18:31–32)

The realization of who we are in Christ and of the full potential of our value changes our perception and allows us to direct our lives to fulfill God's purpose and not our own. God is calling for us to live a bold, fearless life in pursuit of living out His will for us and giving Him all the glory.

Chapter 11
A SERVANT'S HEART

When he had finished washing their feet, he put on his clothes and returned to his place. "Do you understand what I have done for you?" he asked them. "You call me 'Teacher' and 'Lord' and rightly so, for that is what I am. Now that I, your Lord and Teacher, have washed your feet, you also should wash one another's feet. I have set you an example that you should do as I have done for you. Very truly I tell you, no servant is greater than his master, nor is a messenger greater than the one who sent him. Now that you know these things, you will be blessed if you do them."

—John 13:12–17 (NIV)

Having a servant's heart comes with a heart transformation and a desire to live for Christ. Fully surrendering to Christ meant giving up my past transgressions to God and asking for forgiveness. God created us in His image, and that is where our true value and identity lie. As a Christian matures in their faith, the more they strive to become Christlike in everything they do. One of the main components of being more Christlike is having a servant's heart. As Jesus washed the feet of His disciples, so are we to wash the feet of others in service to them.

Part of having freedom in Christ is choosing to serve at a church and serve others. The focus needs to be taken off our self-centered wants and desires and reflected onto helping other people. It is healing to see smiles on other people's faces as you greet them at the door on a Sunday morning or know that you helped make the coffee that is going to help keep people awake during the sermon. It is rewarding to know that no matter what capacity in which we serve, we still have something to offer. It is important to realize that it doesn't matter what we have done in the past; God is a majestic and sovereign god, and He will still use us to help others for His good and faithful will.

We often let our own thoughts of worthlessness get in the way of thinking that we actually have something to offer. Well, we no longer need to listen to those lies. That is how Satan tries to knock us down from having full freedom in Christ. There are so many people out there who need a helping hand, words of encouragement, or just a warm smile to let them know it's going to be okay. We need to start believing in God and trusting that He can use us to serve others not just because we are called to serve but because *past transgressions*.

People recovering from habitual sin have a unique perspective on life. We have seen more than we want to admit and have gone through hell and back, mostly by our own accord. Because of that, we have the special ability to have compassion and empathy toward others who are struggling. We used to be the people that others may have thought were hard to help or approach because we were a little "rough" around the edges. Who better reach out to lost souls that need guidance to see the light of truth than us?

Everyone has something to offer and can learn to have a servant's heart, but the heart must be in the right place. It may take a while to understand the dynamics of serving. I found my way through trial and error. The first time I tried to get back into the good graces of God by serving, I failed miserably. What I once thought was me doing good deeds and serving really became serving my own needs for the attention that I received through that serving.

When I first went back to church years ago, I believed it was the right thing to do. The knowledge was there in my head to go back and find God, so I put one foot in front of the other and decided to fall in line. The problem, as I had stated earlier, was that my head and my heart were not connected. I was there because I knew that was what I was supposed to do, but I was missing the relational component of what it really meant to go to church. Serving was what everyone else was doing at church, so that was what I believed I needed to do.

Since I was good with children, I signed up to be part of the kids' program. I enjoyed being part of the program as I was able to act onstage in skits and help lead the kids in worship and song. I loved every minute of it—only I loved it a little too much. The realization came years later when I came to terms with the fact that my motivation was really all about me and how I felt people perceived me. If everyone saw how much time and effort I put into volunteering, then it was a good thing for me.

Everything I did while serving had a personal benefit in feeding my attention and acceptance complex. If it didn't benefit me, I wouldn't do it. Even as I look back now, I can see that I was not bearing any fruit or blessings from God. Smiles were being put on the children, and they were learning about God, but for myself, I was still dead inside. If we are serving to glorify God rather than ourselves, then we should be able to see the fruit that grows from our efforts. I really had no sense of what it meant to live for Christ. I felt like I had to take part in serving because it is what any Christian would do.

The bottom line was that my heart transformation had not yet occurred, and to serve as Christ did, our hearts must be full of grace, love, humility, and sacrifice. At the time, I was serving so that I could say that I was serving, and it would be put on my resume of things I had done and accomplished. In hindsight, my main motivation in serving was to benefit me and secondarily because I thought the church needed help.

I believed they couldn't afford the staff that it takes to effectively run a church, so that's why volunteers stepped in. That is all true, but I perceived serving as something the church, as a business organization, needed, and not something that Jesus commanded us to do. I was missing the mark on what serving was all about.

> Serve wholeheartedly as if you were serving the Lord, not people. (Ephesians 6:7 NIV)

The key to anything and everything in life is Christ. Every problem this world has can be answered with the words of God. Every situation is intertwined with the next and woven in and out of trials and tribulations, even moments of happiness and joy. All these connections are allowed and masterminded by the one and only Almighty Creator. It still blows my mind that we are His orchestra, and He is the conductor. If we do not follow His lead, the music begins to scramble and becomes noise instead of a beautiful, elegant sound. Until I knew what a relationship with Christ looked like, I wouldn't recognize or understand the true meaning of serving.

Here is an honesty check, if you are serving at a church or any type of organization—what is your motive? Are you serving because it is what Jesus called you to do or because it somehow benefits you either through recognition or a resume booster? Or are you not serving at all because you don't think you are good at anything or worthy of being able to serve?

These are questions I often ask myself. Our hearts naturally drift toward seeking the joy in serving due to a level of acceptance and recognition. At a certain level, it is okay to accept that recognition if you are serving with the right motivation. Perform a heart check to make sure the real reason you serve is for the love of Jesus Christ. And if you are not serving, pray about where you can start and realize that it will glorify God while helping you find a life of freedom in Christ.

> For you were called to freedom, brothers. Only do not use your freedom as an opportunity for the flesh, but through love serve one another. (Galatians 5:13 NIV)

Serving our Lord in what He calls us to do is where we will thrive. If my heart is focused on following Him, then the desire to serve would naturally be there. Thirteen years ago, when I truly and fully surrendered my heart to Christ, my desire to serve without personal benefit caught fire. However, my instinct, perhaps to make up for lost time, was a desire to serve in some big way. I thought, *give me a huge project to do for you, Lord, whatever it is, and I will do it.*

My heart was in the right place, but I had to realize that God has to see that He can trust us with the little things first before He can trust us with the big things. The desire was overwhelming to dive right in, but the Lord kept me at His pace and on His timeline. I started out small, helping at the visitor table where I would answer questions from people who wanted to know more about the church and its activities. I also started to consistently attend a Bible study. As I realized later, His plan was to get me foundationally connected and to start growing in my faith through service to Him.

Eventually, as He started to see me consistently choosing to live a life that strived to glorify Him, He gave me that big project. I knew it had to come from God because it was something beyond what I ever thought I was capable of doing. It is not unusual for God to communicate in this way so that we know without a shadow of a doubt that His hand is in it.

God called me to start up and lead a women's recovery program at our church. I had no clue as to how to do it, but I knew that if I showed up and leaned on His strength, He would use me as His messenger to other women. This was a far stretch from what I used to think. I believed that only people who strive to be perfect Christians in everything they do have the high honor of leading a Bible study. But I soon found out that we are all human and we all make mistakes. It is in our weakness that God uses us to our fullest capability. It is only when we know we are broken and humbled that God can use us as His messenger to help others.

Helping other women has become my heart's passion. It was not until I was fully healed and free that God used my past brokenness to help others. I never imagined that God would want me to serve in this capacity and in such an important role. I simply did not feel worthy. There were days, and there are still days, when I ask God, "Why me?" After all, I am no one in the grand scheme of things. Then I just hear Him tell me in my heart with a loving and stern voice, "Because, my dear child, you have a servant's heart who has surrendered to me. I have given you the strength to fulfill my purposes. You just need to choose to accept that I have chosen you for this role."

My heart skips a beat every time I think about God choosing me for this assignment. But because He chose me, I will trust in Him for strength to make the sacrifices to serve with love and compassion in this ministry to help women become free from habitual sin. There are moments of exhaustion. There are moments of heartbreak when someone just doesn't understand the blessings that come with a life of surrendering to Christ. But there are also moments of blessings in seeing women enter the freedom of life in Christ.

There is always hope for a better life than the one we choose for ourselves. We just have to learn to let go of our past. We need to learn that our value is in Christ and not of this world or what our friends or family think of us, or even what we think of ourselves. We need to choose to lean on God as our Lord and Savior. We need to accept the life Christ has chosen for us and latch onto living a life with a servant's heart. Are you willing to wash the feet of others like Jesus washed the feet of His disciples?

One thing I learned in serving is that no job is too small or too big. Human nature will point out different tasks that we think may be beneath us or tasks that may appear to be overwhelming in work, and we balk at the thought of putting in that many hours. I can tell you from experience that God has chosen each task for each person; it is unique to that person, and we should answer His call every time without fear and without hesitation.

I once had a friend who was getting down on herself because she only helped with the laundry at church. She cleaned the towels and the tablecloths every other week, and she just felt like it wasn't that important or significant. She needed to stop thinking like that, because every job has a purpose, and every job leads to helping others. If the tablecloths were not washed every week, then they would not be ready for the women's

Bible study, where an inviting table helps bring in women to a warm and accepting group of ladies. These tablecloths help set an environment where women accept Christ almost every week, and it all started with washing the tablecloths that help set the tone for a friendly environment.

It reminds me of something someone once said about a mosquito. A mosquito can seem to be small and insignificant. All they do is fly around with no seeming purpose. They could be said to be behind the scenes. They are almost invisible until they decide to start buzzing in and around your ear. You start to notice the mosquito and try to swat it away as it grates on your nerves. Yet the mosquito keeps at it. You must ask yourself, if the mosquito is so small and insignificant, how could it make so much noise to where you start to notice? Just because the task that we may do is considered a small task does not mean that it doesn't make a lot of noise in the end. We may not always see the fruits of our labor, but it's the trust that we have in God, knowing that he will water the seed if we plant it.

Not all of us know what area God is calling us to serve in. Just praying for direction can be quite frustrating, as often silence is all we experience. But don't give up; that silence may be God's way of trying to tell you that you need to do something in parallel with praying. Start trying different areas in your church to serve and see if you feel anything toward that area of service.

Start off small and work your way into different areas. There is something to be said for filling a small need in a church. God gives each of us special spiritual gifts that we can use together as a church body to do good works for God's purposes. It is important that we know what each of our gifts is so that we can help utilize the gifts that God has granted us.

We have different gifts, according to the grace given to each of us. If your gift is prophesying, then prophesy in accordance with your faith; if it is serving, then serve; if it is teaching, then teach; if it is to encourage, then give encouragement; if it is giving, then give generously; if it is to lead, do it diligently; if it is to show mercy, do it cheerfully. (Romans 12:6–8)

A little caveat is in store here: It is important to understand that not all of us will be good at the same thing. Some of us are not called to lead Bible studies, and that's okay. Some of us are not called to serve with children, and that's okay. Some of us are not called to be greeters, and that's okay too. That's why each of us has a special place in the church. Together, we make up the full church body. Know your gifts that God has given you and pray about where God wants you to serve. If you do not know what your spiritual gifts are, you can go to www.spiritualgifttest.com and take the test to find out.

Just as a body, though one, has many parts, but all its many parts forms one body, so it is with Christ. For we were all baptized by one Spirit so as to form one body—whether Jews or Gentiles, slave or free—and we were all given the one Spirit to drink. Even so the body is not made up of one part but of many.

Now if the foot should say, "Because I am not a hand, I do not belong to the body," it would not for that reason stop being part of the body. And if the ear should say, "Because I am not an eye, I do not belong to the body," it would not for that reason stop being part of the body. If the whole body were an eye, where would the sense of hearing be? If the whole body were an ear, where would the sense of smell be? But in fact God has placed the parts in the body, every one of them, just as he wanted them to be. If they were all one part, where would the body be? As it is, there are many parts, but one body.

The eye cannot say to the hand, "I don't need you!" And the head cannot say to the feet, "I don't need you!" On the contrary, those parts of the body that seem to be weaker are indispensable, and the parts that we think are less honorable we treat with special honor. And the parts that are unpresentable are treated with special modesty, while our presentable parts need no special treatment. But God has put the body together, giving greater honor to the parts that lacked it, so that there should be no division in the body, but that its parts should have equal concern for each other. If one part suffers, every part suffers with it; if one part is honored, every part rejoices with it.

Now you are the body of Christ, and each one of you is a part of it. And God has placed in the church first of all apostles, second prophets, third teachers, then miracles, then gifts of healing, of helping, of guidance, and of different kinds of tongues. Are all apostles? Are all prophets? Are all teachers? Do all work miracles? Do all have gifts of healing? Do all speak in tongues? Do all interpret? Now eagerly desire the greater gifts. (1 Corinthians 12:12–30)

Developing a servant's heart has an impact on transforming the heart and leads to healing. Being able to help others, even in something small, helps give the importance and the worth so desperately needed after a past of habitual sin. Serving others builds relationships and provides the connection and accountability lost so long ago when we separated ourselves from Christ in our sinful behavior. It takes the focus off us and puts Jesus Christ at the forefront of our minds.

We are called to love our neighbors and our enemies. We are called to wash people's feet in service as Jesus washed the disciples' feet. Jesus came to us as a servant. His whole purpose on this earth was to be of service to us. He served us in the biggest way possible. He gave His life on the cross to pay the debt of our sins so that we may have a relationship with God. He has the ultimate servant's heart, and I don't know about you, but I want to live and glorify Christ as He sacrificially lived for me. It is time for us to become fearless in our new identities in Christ to fulfill the purpose of bringing people into God's eternal kingdom.

Chapter 12
FEARLESS

We all want progress, but if you're on the wrong road,
progress means doing an about turn and walking back
to the right road; in that case, the man who turns back
soonest is the most progressive.

—C. S. Lewis

I have been on many wrong roads in my life. I am sure I will
probably drift onto many more wrong roads before my time
is up here on this earth. Living a God-fearing life and living it
fearlessly in this world is a hard task, especially in this world
full of darkness. It is important that the light of Christ is
brought back into this world so that people can know what it
is like living a life to glorify Christ.

How is that done? Start by being fearless: in praying, being
obedient, in hope and faith, in surrender, and in love. In other
words, fearless in taking action to live a Christ-filled life no
matter what others think of us. That is the hard part. Too many
of us put too much value into what others think, and we adapt
our identity into what others want and not what we are meant
to be in God's image.

We need to pray for courage so that when we do start to feel
fear or embarrassment, we have the strength to overcome those

emotions. Are you tired of living a life that feels like it has no purpose, a life in which you feel like you are spinning your wheels and getting nowhere?

Fearless Surrender

If you are a control freak like me, this is one of the toughest things to do. Admitting that my way is not always the best way goes against my very nature. I tend to be very impatient, and when I want something, I want it now. Sometimes I try to rationalize taking things into my own hands by telling myself that Jesus must be too busy right now to give me what I want. That's right; I'm just going to help Him out a little bit and take this off His plate. Countless times I ended up making a complete mess. God can move mountains and perform miracles, so what in the world makes me think He is too busy to handle my wants and desires? Often, God is telling me to wait because He is working on something so much better than I ever imagined or He is telling me no because He wants me to go down a different road that will bless my life even more.

I used to think that by fully surrendering to Christ, it was too much of a sacrifice. I felt like I would have to give up so much of my life and must follow all these rules and give up the things that I like doing. It required too much effort on my part. And then, what would my friends think if I became a "Jesus freak" or a "Bible thumper"? Would I lose those friendships? The answer, to my surprise, ended up being quite different. After a few years of fully surrendering to Him, I realized that it is not a sacrifice, but a blessing. Keep in mind that fully surrendering is not as easy as it sounds. To get to that point, I had to learn to let go of my past and my present. This was extremely difficult in that I had become obsessed with trying to fill that empty void inside, obsessed to the point of trying anything and everything to experience that love and fulfillment as I thought it was once defined. It was not until I surrendered to Christ that the emptiness began to fill up with God's love. What I did not understand for so long is that Christ had always accepted me, but I had put up this barrier of self-centered control that quenched God's efforts to reach me. Upon finally realizing this, I felt the truth of His love and felt accepted. I had asked for and understood forgiveness, let go of my past, and forgave myself. I fearlessly surrendered.

If you have not surrendered, it's time to do just that. I promise that your life will be like a wilted flower that has come back to a life full of blessings.

Luke 7 tells a story about a woman who had lived a sinful life and, upon finding out that Jesus was having dinner at a Pharisee's (Simon) house, she went to the house with a jar of perfume.

> As she stood behind Jesus she started weeping and began to wet His feet with her tears and to dry them with her hair. She kissed His feet and then poured the expensive perfume on them. Simon was stunned that Jesus was allowing this sinful woman to touch Him and expressed his dismay.
>
> Jesus told Simon "Two people owed money to a certain moneylender. One owed him five hundred denarii, and the other fifty. Neither of them had the money to pay him back, so he forgave the debts of both. Now which of them will love him more?"
>
> Simon replied, "I suppose the one who had the bigger debt forgiven."
>
> "You have judged correctly," Jesus said.

Then he turned toward the woman and said to Simon, "Do you see this woman? I came into your house. You did not give me any water for my feet, but she wet my feet with her tears and wiped them with her hair. You did not give me a kiss, but this woman, from the time I entered, has not stopped kissing my feet. You did not put oil on my head, but she poured perfume on my feet. Therefore, I tell you, her many sins have been forgiven—as her great love has shown. But whoever has been forgiven little loves little."

Then Jesus said to her, "Your sins are forgiven."

As I read this story, I reflected on my past sins and knew that there were many to forgive. Satan wants us to feel like our sins are too great to be forgiven, but this story demonstrates that the greater the life of sin that has been forgiven, the greater the impact on gratefulness and understanding of the depth of Christ's forgiveness. This, in turn, results in a greater desire to live to glorify Christ. If you have a past like mine, you can be confident and fearless in your pursuit of Christ because no sin is too dark to be forgiven. What a huge relief.

Fearless Hope and Faith

Hope and faith are linked together. Faith believes in a God that is unseen to our naked eye, but that lives within our soul and can be seen in the design of all creation. A fearless faith in Christ means a willingness to take the necessary steps of obedience to pursue the life that God has planned for us. That is the path to a life full of peace and joy. God did not want me to live a life where drugs and sex were my idols, but He sure knew how He could use it for good. You can be that person too. You can be that person who has enough hope and faith that Christ will set you free from your habitual sins. You can be that person that God uses to help others become free through setting an example of a God-centered life. Hope is more than what we think of it in today's terms. We use the word so loosely, but when you intertwine hope with faith it takes on a whole new meaning.

Hope is the confident expectation of joy. I know what some of you may be thinking. It is hard to have hope when there is no end in sight to your pain and struggles. It is hard to see hope when everything in your life seems to be turned upside down. But trust me, the path to freedom is to strive to change your way of thinking. Hope doesn't just mean a feeling of expectation and desire for a certain thing to happen. The word *hope* is often used incorrectly. From the Christian perspective, it really means to look forward to a joy grounded in the gift of eternal life with God. To have hope, you have to have faith, faith in a God who loves you unconditionally, faith in a God who knows you better than yourself and stands next to you in every situation. It is knowing that you have eternal life by having faith in our Lord and Savior: that is hope. It is the hope to keep moving forward no matter what happens in this life because we are working toward eternal life, where there will be no more tears, pain, and suffering. That is where my hope lies. It makes it easier to get through every trial and tribulation that comes my way because no matter what happens, I know through my faith that I have hope and joy in being with Jesus Christ forever.

This is my heart's desire for everyone in this world. If you are a nonbeliever and you are willing to ask Jesus to show you that He is real and can make good on His promises, He will. He is waiting for you to give up control and give it all to Him. When you do, He will show you unconditional love and the joy that it provides. If you are a believer, stop and think about the negativity that you may be allowing in your life, and realign it with the promises of God. Stop asking where God is, and start seeking and acknowledging Him, because He has always been standing right next to you, waiting for you to take His hand.

God is always with us, especially when going through difficult times. But it is important to stop and contemplate what He is doing by allowing us to go through these different situations. What is He orchestrating? I can attest by experience that God will always use a bad situation for good; we may just not see it or understand it at that time, but it is the trust, faith, and hope that we have in Christ that we know He is a good God.

We grow in our relationship with Christ through our brokenness and trials. They are a necessary part of spiritual growth. If nothing but good happens to us, we get complacent and will miss the blessings that God has for us as we go through different trials. In addition, we may also miss out on the opportunity to help someone else with our own experiences. What does it look like to stay anchored in hope?

It means we can forgive as Christ forgave us. We can have joy even through the tough times because we know the outcome is going to be eternal life.

> Consider it pure joy, my brothers and sisters, whenever you face trials of many kinds, because you know that the testing of your faith produces perseverance. (James 1:2–3 NIV)

> We are hard pressed on every side, but not crushed; perplexed, but not in despair; persecuted, but not abandoned; struck down, but not destroyed. We always carry around in our body the death of Jesus, so that the life of Jesus may also be revealed in our body. For we who are alive are always being given

over to death for Jesus' sake, so that his life may also be revealed in our mortal body. So then, death is at work in us, but life is at work in you.

It is written: "I believed; therefore, I have spoken." Since we have that same spirit of faith, we also believe and therefore speak, because we know that the one who raised the Lord Jesus from the dead will also raise us with Jesus and present us with you to himself. All this is for your benefit, so that the grace that is reaching more and more people may cause thanksgiving to overflow to the glory of God.

Therefore, we do not lose heart. Though outwardly we are wasting away, yet inwardly we are being renewed day by day. For our light and momentary troubles are achieving for us an eternal glory that far outweighs them all. So, we fix our eyes not on what is seen, but on what is unseen, since what is seen is temporary, but what is unseen is eternal. (2 Corinthians 4:8–18 NIV)

Fearless Obedience

To be obedient means to have enough belief in Christ to follow Him without question. This requires mounds of faith and trust that God's plans and purposes for us are perfect. A few years back, I started what I call my faith bucket. I began it because I realized that hindsight is twenty-twenty in understanding our past experiences. Every time I saw God working in my life, I took the memory of His good works and what He did for me and put it in my faith bucket. Then, when I felt God calling me to do something that seemed too scary, I pulled out the faith bucket and started reviewing the mounds of memories. This process reminded me of God's faithfulness and that He will continue to be faithful in the new calling.

God has been calling me to do a lot over these last couple of years. Sometimes, they were small things, which seemed easy enough to obey, and some things were big. It has been the big things that often seemed completely beyond my abilities, where I would find myself lost in what to do. However, I have learned that when I felt this sense of feeling lost, it was an indicator that the leading was from God. The only way for His will to be followed was for me to lean completely on Him and let Him do His thing through me. One of those big things was to call me to minister to women who struggle in all aspects of life. Another was when He called me to quit my job and give up my financial security and a bonus. Then He called me to lead a Bible study for women. These are all examples of His callings that, to be honest, scared the daylight out of me and ignited severe insecurities.

The conversations that I had with God on these very issues were very intense. It would go something like this, "I can't, Lord, there is no way," and God would respond, through an understanding in my heart, that this isn't something meant for me to do within my own strength. It is meant for me to do in His strength so that it glorifies Him. The process of Him calling me to something, then my resistance, and then ultimately surrendering to His leading and obedience to His will changed my life for the better. The blessings that God has given to me because of my obedience go beyond what I ever thought possible.

Following Christ is not just going to church on Sunday and saying that you believe. It requires us to act upon our faith to fulfill God's purpose for our lives, which is, ultimately, to share God's light with others and bring them to Christ. We are meant to be far greater than anything we could conjure up for ourselves in this lifetime. It is time to be fearless in our obedience and be willing to fearlessly jump in the name of Christ. Our lives are so much better when we follow what our Almighty Creator has planned for us instead of our own plans. Are you willing to jump with me in faith and obedience and see where God takes you?

Fearless Prayer

When we accept Christ as Lord and Savior, we are changed forever as a child of God. But that is just the beginning of our growth and maturing in Him. A critical component of growing and maturing in Him is to be regularly on our knees praying. This is such a crucial step in changing from the old self to a new self in Christ. It is important to finally say "Enough is enough," and realize that we can't handle things on our own strength.

When we are willing to admit that we are inadequate, then we open our hearts to let Christ in. Without prayer, our relationship with God will be stagnant. You may as well have no relationship.

Many people do not know how to pray and are intimidated by it. They feel like they have to have just the right words in order to reach God. It is not like that; prayer is just a simple conversation between you and God. There is no right or wrong way to pray. If you have no idea how to pray, simply start by saying "Lord, I need your help," and tell Him what's on your mind.

Prayer is one of the most important steps in strengthening our walk with Christ. Yet it is often taken for granted. Most people tend to pray as a last resort when they have a massive problem and only after they have exhausted all their own problem-solving ideas. Or they tend to pray for other people and not for themselves. Praying for these things is not wrong as God hears all our prayers, but it is important to remember to pray fearlessly not only during the bad times but also during the good times.

We need to live with a heart of gratitude and thankfulness. We also need to pray for ourselves. When I ask for prayer requests during Bible study, I always tell people to put down a request for someone else and then put down a request for themselves. Most people tend to think that other people's struggles are more important than their own little problems and so tend not to pray for themselves. I'll tell you a little secret. God wants us to spill our guts with what happens during each day. He wants to hear what problems we are facing and what blessings we have received. That is exactly what a relationship is all about. He wants to simply hear about our day.

We can only begin to touch the sky of heaven when our knees are hitting the ground. It isn't until we start to pray fervently that we begin to see changes in our behavior and our lives. It causes a ripple effect. Putting time aside to pray each day brings us closer to God and fills us with a sense of peace and joy in our daily walk with Him. Over time, others start to notice the subtle changes in us, and they begin to want the same experience. And it all starts with prayer.

Every day should start with prayer. One thing I learned to do over the last few years was not only spill my day and worries to God, but also to thank Him for everything that He has done for me. I have learned to be specific in my prayers, as well. The more specific we are in our prayers, the more we can see God working within our prayers and how he answers them.

Another critical factor is to listen. Many people think that prayer is a one-way dialogue with God, but it goes both ways.

God speaks to our hearts, but the problem for a lot of people is they do not know how to be quiet and listen during their prayer time. It is not difficult but may take some practice. It is hard to just be still and tune in to the voice of God in our hearts. But trust me, it is real, and it works.

Start trying to think of yourself as a prayer warrior with the goal of building a relationship with Christ. Oh, and one more thing, when I talk about being on your knees, it does not always mean figuratively. God listens to us at all times of the day and in all circumstances. He is just a thought and a word away. All you must do is acknowledge Him and speak like He is physically standing right next to you. It is that real.

Fearless Love

To love means to be vulnerable, opening your heart and allowing people to be close. It's straight-up terrifying, if you ask me, but it wasn't always that way. In my journey, I went from wanting love so badly that I would do anything to get it, to getting my heart broken so many times that I shut it down, sealed it in a box, and used superglue to seal it shut. I went from one extreme to the other.

It wasn't until I fully surrendered to Christ that I slowly started to unseal that box and let my heart breathe a little. But it was a slow process because I feared getting hurt, and I didn't want to go through the pain of heartbreak again. When I think about it, I could probably have lived my life with my heart sealed up forever, but what kind of life would that have been?

God wants us to have a quality life. He calls us to love because He is love. He is the standard and embodiment of love. His very character is love. And since He created us in His image, He also created us to love and be loved. We are wired for relationships. If I had continued to live with my heart sealed in a superglued box, I would have missed out on the blessings of having a true relationship with Christ.

During those times when my heart was severely broken, I didn't have Christ in my life. But once I learned to love Christ and accept His love, love itself didn't seem so scary. I found myself opening up again, building friendships, and my life began to fill up with blessings. We need to love one another in this world.

To truly learn to love and allow us to be loved, we need to remove the masks we often hide behind. I used to wear them too. I would change my personality depending on whom I was with, so no one really knew the real me. If people don't know the real us, how can they love us for who we truly are? This takes courage.

Overcoming the fear of taking off the masks and letting people know that we are imperfect and may have baggage takes a lot of bravery. But love heals all. When we start to love others outwardly and unconditionally, we begin to see that perhaps others can love us just as we are too. And that opens the door to allow us to love ourselves as who we are in Christ. It also allows us to show others how to love and be vulnerable, as well.

*****

I don't know where you are in life right now. Maybe you are amid a painful struggle and realize that you are using substances to cope with and ease the pain. Maybe you are searching for that quick fix to make you feel better and find yourself in a vicious cycle from which there seems to be no way out. Maybe you are enslaved to negative thoughts that constantly tear you down. Or maybe, as you read this, you realize that you know someone who is going through something similar. My hope is that you can take my story and know that there is a light at the end of the tunnel.

No longer do we need to be slaves to our fear of being hopelessly inadequate and purposeless in life. It is not until we find the courage to be fearless in the pursuit of Christ and to seek Him that we will start to live the life that God has planned for us. Rick Warren once said, "The greatest tragedy is not death itself, it is living a life without purpose."

There is no sin too great for Jesus to forgive. If Christ can forgive someone like me after my countless sins and all I have done to disgrace Him, then He can forgive you too. All you must do is ask. Maybe you feel like you are in a pitch-black room and there is no light to find your way. I pray that my story can be that flashlight in your dark room.

My hope is for you to be inspired to act. Take control of your life and lay your burdens at God's feet. He is longing for a close relationship with you, and He is longing to provide healing for you. He is just waiting for you to surrender to Him. We are called to action in living a life that glorifies Christ. Let's take our brokenness and let God use it for good. Let God rescue you as He has rescued me.

Blessings

After writing this book and being obedient to the Lord, God brought my husband, Shawn, into my life. Believe it or not, I had sworn off online dating, but I kept getting this feeling that God wanted me to try eHarmony again. I denied it for a long time, not wanting to have to go through all the awkwardness of dating and weeding through all the different profiles. But God kept confirming it. He sent me ads for discounted plans, and my friends kept telling me I should do it. So, I begrudgingly signed back up. I even expanded my search to open the distance of the search. I wasn't just going to look locally anymore, because if God had someone for me, He would work out the logistics. Lo and behold, one of my first matches were Shawn. I smiled at him online, hoping he would smile back. He did.

He was on an extended vacation up in Canada but lived in Northern California. Had I not listened to God calling me to sign back up and expand my search on the distance, I would have lost out on meeting my soulmate. Within one of the first conversations we had, I told him to read my book then come back to me and let me know if he was still interested. Shawn was surprised when I just let him know my entire life up front, but he later told me that God gave him this overwhelming peace about me. Shawn wasn't worried about my past, but he knew God told him that I am a completely new creation in God and that it would be okay.

Shawn's parents even lived in San Diego, so after a month of talking on the phone, he drove down to his parents and took me out. He planned out the whole date, taking me on a whale-watching boat, dinner, and ice cream after. I had never had anyone really take the time to create a perfect day for me. It was just perfect. After dinner and ice cream, he asked if he could fly me out to Northern California. I was so shocked that he would be willing to pay for a flight for me. He was even going to get me a hotel. Staying at his place was completely out of the picture. I was doing things right this time. It just so happened that I have an aunt who lived just ten minutes away from him, so I was able to stay with her. God had lined up everything perfectly. That was just the beginning.

My husband is a forensic scientist for the State of California, so there are multiple locations in the state. He currently worked in the Sacramento lab at the time God brought us together; however, a year prior to even meeting me, the Riverside lab needed a technical leader to help. Shawn was already coming down to Southern California once a month for a few days. God was lining everything up for when we did get married. Shawn could easily transfer over to Riverside, and I wouldn't have to move.

Five months after we had officially met, Shawn asked me to marry him. I said *yes!* Without any hesitation, I knew everything was of God's plan. The Lord blessed me with an amazing husband. Five months after I had my dream wedding, we were pregnant with our first child. We now have a son, who is six, and our daughter, who is four and a half.

What an amazing gift God has done for me and my family. I thank the Lord every day for the journey he had me go through. God allowed me to go through all those dark times because He knew I would be obedient and use my past to help others. He knew I would follow Him with all my heart, and He blessed me with my heart's desires.

Following God is so much more than just being of service. It fills me up with peace and joy. I have a heart of gratitude, and I can't thank God enough for loving me unconditionally. He is good and so ever faithful. I can't wait to one day meet my Lord and Savior face-to-face and have Him tell me, "Well done, my good and faithful servant."

Epilogue

When God called me to write this book, I immediately told Him there was no way. I am an accountant. I work with numbers all day, primarily because I did not do well with English in school. It was a constant battle for me to write papers and express myself through words. This was completely beyond me. God and I went back and forth for about six months until He gave me confirmation after confirmation that He was calling me to put my story down on paper. I had no other choice but to follow His lead and be obedient to His calling for me. With fear in my soul, I started to write.

Writing my story required me to be vulnerable and transparent to a point that pushed my boundaries and exceeded my comfort levels, yet I continued to write. This was a definite learning experience for me, and I know that I have grown in my faith throughout this process. There were times when I typed on my keyboard as tears welled up in my eyes and poured down my cheeks as I pushed myself to revisit a very dark time.

Even though there were moments of sadness, there were also moments of feeling completely overwhelmed with God's love and the peacefulness that comes with understanding what Christ did for me. He pulled me out of my muddy pit not once, but several times, and still said "I love you." His unconditional love pulled me through and pushed me toward true freedom. God's grace is what got me to where I am today, and only by His love am I the person He has called me to be.

My hope is that my story will inspire you to act, whatever that may be for you. It may mean deciding that you want a relationship with Christ. Or it may be that you want to recommit your life to Christ and get back on track. Whatever you feel that call to action may be for you, my hope is that you know that there is hope for a better life than what you could have ever imagined with our Lord and Savior, Jesus Christ. May in your weakness and your brokenness you allow Jesus to use you in His purpose. Let's shine God's light on an imperfect and dark world because in the end, it is not this world that we live for, but eternal life with Jesus Christ.

If you have never prayed the prayer to accept Jesus into your life and you would like to, it is very easy. Below is a prayer of salvation that you can pray. If you decide to pray this prayer, may I just say congratulations on making the first step to a brand-new life and a brand-new you. I will be praying for you, and I am so excited for you.

If you are in the position of already accepting Christ earlier in your life but have lost your way, I pray that you decide to recommit your life to Christ, for He is the only way, the truth, and the life. Below is a prayer of recommitment that may help you get right with God.

Prayer of Salvation

Dear heavenly Father, I know that I am a sinner, Lord, and I understand that You sent Your only son to die on the cross for my sins. Please forgive me for not living a life that glorified You. I want to spend the rest of my life in Your kingdom, Lord, and I know that it requires repentance and me turning from my sin. With Your help and strength, I believe I can leave my old life behind me. I want to transform my old self into a new self that lives a life for Your purpose, Lord, and not my own. I ask that You fill me with the power of the Holy Spirit so that I may be Your child. Amen.

Prayer of Recommitment

Lord, I have strayed far from the path of righteousness, and I ask that You forgive me. I realize now that taking control of my life has not benefited me, and it is far from what You want for me. I know that You love me, Lord, and I want to recommit myself to living a life that glorifies You. Please give me the strength and wisdom to turn from my sins and rebuild my relationship with You. The last thing I want is to be separated from You, and my past choices have led me away. Transform my heart to desire to be close to You, Lord, as I want to be right with You. Amen.

We are all continuous works in progress and will be until our work is done on this earth. We will continue to go through trials and tribulations throughout our life, but with God on our side, we can get through those struggles a little bit easier, still with the peace and comfort of knowing where our eternal home will be. I pray that you live a life that shines God's light and realize that our purpose here on earth is to help bring others to Christ and to show His love through our actions. Let's live boldly on faith and put our faith into action, because being rescued inspires rescuing. We can now be the rescuers.

Light at the End of the Tunnel
Courtney Kacer

Falling full of darkness
Wish I was unconscious
Full of mixed emotions
Complete at my lowness
Trying to dig deep for joy, but all I do is destroy
Looking for love in all the wrong places
I can't remember all their faces
All I want to do is cope
And I keep thinking there is no hope
Right when I am about to quit
Jesus dug me out of my pit
A light at the end of the tunnel shone bright
Even thought it was the dead of night
He gave me hope to continue on
Little by little I turned into a swan
Darkness turned into a bright, shiny light
And now I am standing upright
A light at the end of the tunnel shone bright
Because Jesus filled me with pure delight

Milton Keynes UK
Ingram Content Group UK Ltd.
UKHW010615250624
444652UK00001B/77